D1448635

Broad Street

E H NEW

BLACKWELL'S
1879–1979

BLACKWELL'S
1879–1979

THE HISTORY OF A FAMILY FIRM

———

A. L. P. NORRINGTON

BLACKWELL · OXFORD

© B. H. Blackwell Ltd.
Broad Street, Oxford

First published 1983
Reprinted 1985

British Library Cataloguing in Publication Data

Norrington, A. L. P.
Blackwell's 1879–1979
1. B. H. Blackwell Limited
I. Title
381'450705'0942574   Z325
ISBN 0-946344-00-0

.

Printed in Great Britain
at the University Press, Oxford
by David Stanford
Printer to the University

TO

RICHARD BLACKWELL

IN GRATEFUL MEMORY OF

HIS LIFE AND WORK

Foreword

Books about family firms are apt to furnish scant entertainment to readers other than those immediately concerned with them, but this centenary history of Blackwell's may, I hope, prove exceptional. Written by the lively hand of Sir Arthur ('Thomas') Norrington, one-time Secretary to the Delegates of the Oxford University Press, it tells the story of the bookshop, founded by my father with one apprentice in 1879, which now has a staff of over 600 and, having generated its necessary capital out of its own profits, remains a private family firm. It has been its good fortune down the years to attract the services of men—and presently women—of rare character and ability. So has been engendered a spirit of mutual respect ripening into mutual loyalty between management and staff so that what might have been a paternalist regime is in effect an informal society dedicated to guiding worthy books into worthy hands.

Only one major misfortune has befallen the firm in the course of its constant growth; this was the death in 1980 of Richard Blackwell in his 62nd year. Under the immense ability of his chairmanship the firm made massive progress. His best bequest to the firm are his two sons Miles and Nigel, who with my son Julian and grandson Philip furnish assurances that Blackwell's will remain a private enterprise.

BASIL BLACKWELL

April 1983

Contents

x _Contents_

List of Illustrations

List of Illustrations

Acknowledgements

We owe thanks to Roger Cole, John Cutforth, Christopher Francis and many others who contributed advice and information as the book took shape; to Ken Stewart, late of the Oxford University Press, who designed it; to the *Oxford Mail*, who generously allowed us to reproduce the photographs on pages 91, 126, 154, 157, 159, 169, 176, and 180; to Stella Harris for her portrait on page 141; and to Blackstone New York for the portrait of Richard Blackwell on page 141.

BENJAMIN HENRY BLACKWELL

I

The Birth of a Bookshop

WHEN Benjamin Henry Blackwell opened his shop at No. 50 Broad Street, Oxford, on New Year's Day, 1879, he was fulfilling a resolve made by his mother more than twenty years earlier. Her husband, Benjamin Harris Blackwell, had set up as a bookseller in 1845 at 46 High Street, St. Clement's. The rent of this small property, where his neighbours on either side were William Loder, Pork Butcher, and Samuel Prince, Baker, was £18 a year.[1] Blackwell chose this site, just outside the City's eastern boundary, as it then was, because only Freemen, and their sons and apprentices, could set up a new business in the city itself without payment of a fine. Five other shopkeepers, in protest against this restrictive practice, established their businesses beyond Magdalen Bridge at about the same time. Only one, Henry Eagleston, who combined the callings of ironmonger and straw-hat-maker, survived this detachment from the commercial centre. His family continued to trade successfully, though latterly only as ironmongers, until 1947.

Benjamin Blackwell was in his thirty-second year, and had only ten more years to live. Very busy years they must have been, with a business to establish and, in due course, a wife and family to provide for. He traded almost exclusively in second-hand books, and he certainly compiled catalogues to stimulate their sale, for a bill survives dated 11 January 1853, detailing work done for him, at a total cost of £1. 14s. 6d., by the *Oxford Chronicle* on the preparation and production of 250 catalogues of 12 pages each. Steamboats were by then

[1] The Oxford Directory of 1846 lists Benj. Blackwell, Bookseller, among the 22 then in business, one of them 'Fred Trash', whose name was marked with an asterisk signifying 'also a publisher'.

able to cross the Atlantic in a fortnight, so there may be a direct connection between the issue of this catalogue and a letter which he received some twenty weeks later (on 30 May 1853) from a Mr John Gooch of Pennsylvania. Addressed to 'My dear Benj. H.B.', the letter thanks the bookseller for his parcel of books 'which almost without exception please' and encloses a money order for £4. 14s. 0d. in payment, 'much wishing you increase of profitable business'. The promotion of trade with America, and the cultivation of good service to customers, were already Blackwellian features in the year that saw the outbreak of the Crimean War.

The business and the family were not the only calls on Benjamin Blackwell's time, and care. He and his brother, Isaac Harris Blackwell, were founding members of the Oxford Teetotal Society, a cause no doubt commended to them by their father, who had become a total abstainer to mark his disapproval of the Government by depriving it of his contribution to the excise duty. The Society maintained a reading room furnished with temperance and other periodicals, and a lending library of standard works, and Benjamin Harris acted as librarian. This experience may have prompted him to apply for the post of librarian in the new City of Oxford Public Library, opened in June 1854 in the old (pre-1893) Town Hall. He was the first Oxford City Librarian, and his duties were thus laid down by the Committee; 'A Librarian and an assistant have been appointed, whose duty it will be to be in attendance at all times, during the week-days, from 9 in the morning till 11 in the evening in Summer, and from 9 till 10 in Winter, and from 6 in the evening till 10 on Sundays.' For this 88-hour week (but only 82 in the winter) the Librarian was paid £60 a year and his assistant 7d. a week. The Library at this early stage was simply a reference library and reading room, and the duties largely vigilatorial. It could sometimes, no doubt, be manned (or boyed) by the assistant alone, young Harry Collins.

Was Benjamin Blackwell really thinking of giving up his bookselling business to live on £60 a year? In Trollope's *Framley Parsonage* (1861) Mr Crawley, before he became Vicar of Hogglestock at £130 a year, had somehow lived on £70 a year—with a wife and four children—in a Cornish curacy. He certainly moved himself and his family to 3 Turl Street in 1854, perhaps to be nearer to the Library. We shall never know how it would all have worked out, for within six months he died in his new home, of his old enemy angina pectoris, a frugal hard-working, God-fearing, uncomplaining man. The story is handed down in the family of how, when a sudden stab of pain made him cry out sharply, he would try to forestall his wife's alarm by pretending that his cry was the top note of a scale, and sing the other seven notes downwards. He left a widow and three young children, Benjamin Henry (Harry), the eldest, aged 6, Mathilda, and Frederick. The breadwinner was dead, and the business must be wound up, but there were good friends to stand by her. One of them was a bookseller, Charles Richards, who shared his premises at 104 High Street (formerly the Salutation Inn) with a wine merchant, but that had not, it seems, interfered with his friendship with the Librarian of the Oxford Teetotal Society. He undertook the valuation of the stock (£153. 5s. 0d. for probate) and used his good offices to explain Mrs Blackwell's situation to the publishers to whom the estate owed money. Routledge and Co. generously wrote to surrender their claims against the business 'for Mrs. Blackwell's use—and only regret that she should have been so badly provided for'.

Mrs Blackwell, born Nancy Stirling Lambert, was a determined and courageous young woman, and she set to work to support her family. She left Turl Street and moved to a site near the Canal, and there she began to put her skill as a needlewoman to good account. It was not long before she had apprentice pupils working with her on vestments for the clergy and sprigged waistcoats, then very fashionable, for the undergraduates. Her firm hope was that the name of 'B. H. Blackwell, Bookseller' would one day be revived in her elder son. So, in 1862, when Harry was 13, he left Price's School in Clarendon Street—to his lasting regret—and was bound apprentice to friendly Charles Richards, at one shilling a week, with annual increments of one shilling. He had for some years been a chorister in Queen's College Choir and was thus able to supplement the family's income if only by a little until his voice broke. At Richards's he learned his trade, and when his term was up he was sent to manage a branch of the business at 38 High Street. There was little doing there, and he soon sought fuller scope for his energy and ambition as assistant in the more flourishing firm of Slatter and Rose at 2–3 High Street.

The family fortunes now grew much brighter. Mrs Blackwell moved to 46 Holywell, a house large enough to enable her to let three sets of lodgings in term-time. Harry was earning good money, for those days, with a salary that rose, by 1878, to 40s. a week; enough for him to pay his mother 12s. 6d. a week, enjoy himself as an oarsman and musician, and put by money for the future as well. Brother Frederick was to do well too. He eventually took up a position as Collector of the Water Rate at a salary of £160 a year. Mathilda went off, in 1874, 'for conscience sake', to teach in schools at Bloemfontein in the Orange Free State.

In 1877 Benjamin Henry began to keep a diary. 'I have now been with Mr. Rose six years and seem likely to stay at any rate for another two, at the end of which I hope to be able with a little assistance to open in London or elsewhere a business on my own account.' Like Pip's friend Herbert Pocket in *Great Expectations*, he was beginning to 'look about him' for an opening. He had not, in fact, even been sure that he should become a bookseller, for in 1876 he had seen the post of Librarian of Cardiff advertised, and had applied for it. He was turned down by the selection committee— little did they know what a momentous decision they had made— but a year later he was evidently still thinking of a career away from Oxford.

But Oxford it was to be, not least, perhaps, because of his enthusiastic involvement in other activities there, especially rowing and music. He was a member, and treasurer, of the Falcon Boat Club 'which costs me 24/- per ann.' The club was in great form in 1877. '25 June. Down river in evening—picked crews for sports. In Quelch's four—Annis's said to be the best and Woodward's next (three fours in all). 28 June. Off to Sports 2 p.m. 1st heat, 3 o'clock, beat Annis's easily, very pleased, got plated cup. To Iffley to supper (3/-) songs and toasts till 11; home by boat 12—a very jolly day altogether. I am talked of for the Regatta.' There was music on the river too. '30 July. Orpheus Water Party—1.15 off from shop— started 2 p.m. to Nuneham and back to Sandford to tea, singing all day—very jolly.' He must have been one of the first choristers at SS Philip and James, the new parish church of North Oxford by G. E. Street[1] completed in 1862, for he recorded in 1877 that he had sung there 'for nearly fifteen years'. There was much music-making at home, too, and with friends.

Harry Blackwell was no doubt an exceptional person. Not every-one who worked the normal ten hours a day or more for six full days fitted as much more into the week as he did. To do so needed physical stamina and intelligence and a sort of purposeful simplicity. It was also, to be sure, easier to be 'jolly', the diarist's word for sociably happy, without benefit of television and motor car. Your diversions were home-made, and if their quantity was less than today's, we may envy their quality.

By the end of 1877 his mind was made up. 'Decided this day (12 November) that I will begin business in Oxford and probably in October/79 all going on well'. The matter was settled even sooner. In the following autumn he had found premises that he thought would suit him at 50 Broad Street, and there he decided to set up shop. He could not have chosen a better site, despite the pre-sence of two well-established booksellers further west, on the other side of the road, Parker's and Thornton's. The Sheldonian Theatre, ceremonial centre of the university, was just across the road, next to the Clarendon Building, eponymous home of the University Press from 1713 to 1839, and later, for more than a century, the Univer-sity's administrative headquarters. Behind them lay the Bodleian Library—and some sixty years later the New Bodleian was to be built almost next door to No. 50. He was setting up shop at the heart of the University, though not everyone thought that No. 50 was quite the right place. When he visited Macmillans in London to open an account, Frederick Macmillan's comment was, 'Very well,

---

[1] George Edmund Street (1824–81), honorary architect of the diocese of Oxford, excelled in the building of parish churches; famous as architect of the Law Courts in the Strand; buried in Westminster Abbey.

BROAD STREET, EARLY 1900'S

Mr Blackwell, we shall be pleased to open an account with you but I fear you have chosen the wrong side of the street to be successful'.

The original Blackwell's was a small part of No. 50, the 'shop and back room, with use of cellar, at a rent of £2 a month'. The shop measured 12 ft. by 12 ft., the back room 15 ft. by 12 ft. Here young Blackwell set out his stock of 'Secondhand Books in Ancient and Modern Literature'. He had been buying steadily out of his savings and had managed to accumulate about 700 books, which he valued, conservatively, at £110. This was his working capital, supplemented by a loan from a friend of the family, Mrs Teresa Messer of Thame, with whom he had spent his summer holidays as a boy. The loan was for £150 at three per cent, from which he laid out £70 on a further selection of new and second-hand books, spent £20 on fixtures and fittings for the shop, and kept £60 in reserve. A modest beginning, but he had a fund of experience to draw upon, after seventeen years in the trade. Working hours were long a century ago, six full days a week till late in the evening, though some were shorter than others. 'Business rather slack' he had written in 1877, 'got away soon after 8.' At Richards's branch it had often been very slack indeed, and the young manager had used the empty intervals to address himself to the study, and in large measure the memorizing, of Bernard Quaritch's 1864 *Catalogue of Books, comprising all departments of Literature, many of them rare, valuable and curious,* over 10,000 of them. Years later he would find a book in his hand which he had not seen before, and there would flash back to his memory the description of it in that astonishing record of the stock of the greatest of Victorian booksellers.[1]

Blackwell's own 'catalogue No. 1' has been preserved, and was reprinted for limited circulation in 1973, to coincide with the issue of the firm's catalogue No. 1000. Not surprisingly, Classics lead the field, with a number of standard nineteenth-century texts, grammars, and dictionaries in regular use in the University, and a few fine earlier editions, including two Aldines (5s. and 5s. 6d.) and a Baskerville (5s.). More than two-thirds of the items in the catalogue are priced at 5s. or less, and only forty-five at £1 or more, most of them works in two or more volumes. The large section of books about Oxford includes Loggan's *Oxonia Illustrata* (1675), at £5 the most expensive single volume in the whole catalogue. Two items that would have been even better investments are Piranesi's *Le antichità romane* (1756) in four volumes at £5. 10s. 0d. and the first edition of Hobbes's *Leviathan* (1651) at 18s.: the retail value of these two is now at least a thousand times as high. Item 230, published in 1654 and marked VERY RARE, catches the eye: Thomas Hall's *The Loathesomenesse of Long Haire, or, Treatise wherein you have the Question stated, &c., with the concurrent judgement of Divines, both old and new, against it; with an Appendix against Painting, Spots, Naked Backs, &c.,* 8s. 6d.

---

[1] Bernard Quaritch (1819–99), born in Saxony, commenced bookseller in London 1847; 'developed the most extensive trade in old books in the world' (*DNB*); founder member of 'The Sette of Odd Volumes' dining club.

The business got off to a good start. In 1879 turnover was £1,267. 2s. 11d., rising in the second year to £1,841. 9s. 3d., and showing at the end of 1880 a profit of £226. 10s. 0d. 'Well, Mr Blackwell,' said Mr John Parsons of the Old Bank in High Street, at the end of 1880, 'are you beginning to capture your rivals' trade?' 'I believe', he replied, 'that there is room for all.'

CATALOGUE

OF

SECOND-HAND BOOKS

IN

𝕬ncient and 𝕸odern 𝕷iterature;

Comprising many that are Curious and Scarce, and
a number of valuable and interesting Books relating
to Oxford, including the works of Loggan, Williams,
Skelton, Ingram, and others; being a portion of
the Stock of

B. H. BLACKWELL,

On Sale at exceptionally Low Prices for Cash, at

50, BROAD STREET, OXFORD;

(Opposite the Sheldonian Theatre).

2d.
in the
1/.
Discount
for Cash
off
New Books
published at
2/6
and
upwards.

Libraries
and
Small
Collections
of
Books
Bought
for
Cash.

Second-hand and Scarce Books, not in Stock, sought and advertised
for free of charge.

ORDERS BY POST PROMPTLY ATTENDED TO.

BLACKWELL'S CATALOGUE NO. I

II

The Age of Reform

BENJAMIN HENRY BLACKWELL grew up in a University and Cathedral city surrounded by little villages—Marston, Headington, Cowley, Iffley, Botley—separated from the city, and from each other, by open country. There was no building along the Iffley Road after the first 200 yards beyond Magdalen Bridge, none along the Seven Bridges Road until one reached Botley. The only aid to local transport was the horse. The safety bicycle was not invented until 1888, and cycling did not become popular until the nineties, when Dunlop invented the pneumatic tyre.

The University population was very small. When the first Royal Commission was appointed in 1850 there were no more than 1300 undergraduates, and, like the Fellows, they lived inside their colleges. That had been the rule since the Laudian Statutes of 1636, but the Commissioners' recommendation to enlarge the University in order to admit 'more men from the middle classes' led inevitably to its abolition, not without protests from the critics. 'The notion of men living in lodgings, outside the range of College discipline and deprived of the benefits of compulsory chapel, filled them with decided alarm.'[1]

The Fellows, too, were soon to be free to live outside their colleges. Until the rule of celibacy began to be relaxed in the seventies the best hope for a bachelor in Holy Orders impatient for matrimony was a vacancy in a College living. The new freedom led to the development of 'North Oxford', and St. John's, the fortunate owners of most of the area, gave the names of its College livings to many of the new roads, Bardwell, Belbroughton, Charlbury, and so on,

[1] V. H. H. Green, *An Oxford Common Room* (Arnold, 1957).

where imposing Victorian houses were built to house the academic colonists and their numerous children and servants. When Sir Charles Oman went up from Winchester to New College as a freshman in 1878 he recalled that the invasion had got as far as Canterbury Road, though still, beyond it, was nothing but farms and market gardens until you came to the 'newly erected village' of Summertown.

It was not only in North Oxford that the builders were busy. There was as yet no 'Science Area' but a start had been made with the University Museum in 1855, and, three years after Blackwell opened his shop, the new Examination Schools in High Street were completed. These were designed, in the handsome but not wholly convenient Elizabethan style of Kirby Hall in Northamptonshire, by Sir Thomas Jackson, the most popular architect of his day in Oxford. As the University grew in numbers in obedience to the Royal Commissioners, several colleges put up new buildings at the end of the century. Jackson was responsible for those at Brasenose, Corpus, Hertford, Lincoln, and Trinity—to say nothing of the Oxford High School for boys, the Oxford High School for girls, the remodelling of the spire of St. Mary's (the University church), the University cricket pavilion, and the organ case in the Sheldonian Theatre.

It was in a city where Dr Johnson would have noticed few changes, and in the centre of a University only recently emerging from the complacent torpor in which he had found it, that Blackwell set up in business. There were already more than twenty booksellers in Oxford and here was a young man expecting to make a living as yet one more. But it was the age of small businesses. Wages were low, food and housing were cheap, income tax was 5d. in the pound; and the English believed in, and the middle classes, certainly, practised, the virtues of self-control, self-improvement, and self-denial, virtues mockingly admired in Clough's *Dipsychus*:

> Staid Englishmen, who toil and slave
> From your first breeching to the grave,
> And seldom spend and always save,
> And do your duty all your life
> By your young family and wife.

The bookselling trade in England, as a whole, was in the doldrums in 1879, but the last quarter of the century was to prove a favourable time in which to set up a new business. Whole generations of children were growing up literate for the first time in English history. Forster's Elementary Education Act of 1870 made provision for an elementary school to be placed within reach of every child. Ten years later, when the schools had been built, school attendance was made compulsory. The nationwide extension of secondary education was not to begin until the next century, but there had already been an increase in the provision for sons of the well-to-do. In the twenty-one years between 1841 (Cheltenham) and 1862 (Clifton, Hailey-bury, and Malvern) more than a dozen new public schools were founded. The report of the Public School Commission of 1863 was producing a long-overdue broadening of their curricula, and the grammar schools were following suit. Equally, or more, significant was the growth of secondary education for girls, pioneered in the fifties by Miss Buss and Miss Beale of immortal memory. The Girls' Public Day Schools Trust began in the seventies to establish first-grade schools all over the country. Their Oxford High School was founded in 1875.

The Universities, too, were on the move, as we have seen. The University Tests Act of 1871 abolished the anachronistic regulations that had hitherto excluded dissenters and Roman Catholics from Oxford and Cambridge (J. H. Newman was elected the first honorary fellow of Trinity College, Oxford, in 1877, and two years later was created Cardinal), and the second Royal Commission (of 1876) led to the introduction of new subjects into the curriculum. The two ancient universities were no longer the only degree-granting institutions in England. Durham and London had been founded in the thirties and Manchester was to follow in 1880. The new girls' secondary schools were the signal for the infiltration of women into Oxford and Cambridge. Lady Margaret Hall and Somerville both opened their doors in Oxford in the same year as Blackwell's new bookshop.

These great reforms and advances in education, in the country at large and in Oxford in particular, were to lead to a notable increase in the demand for books. More people began to read more books on more subjects. Religion was still the favourite field with the publishers in 1875, but the subjects in the 'new learning'—history, economics, science—were overhauling the leader. Between 1870 and 1885 the output of new books in these fields more than doubled while religion began to fall back. It was a great time, too, for popularizing knowledge, and taking stock of it. Plato and Homer were made more widely familiar by new translations now long famous. Burton's *Arabian Nights* was published in 1885, and 'revised for household reading' two years later. J. R. Green's *Short History of the English People* (1875) was enormously popular. The most famous of all large-scale reference-books, the *Oxford English Dictionary* and the *Dictionary of National Biography*, began to appear in the eighties. The earliest use of the phrase 'the general reader' recorded by the former is dated 1862.

Poetry was entering a long decline in output and popularity. Nearly all Tennyson's best work had been published before 1875, and after his death in 1892 the early verse of Bridges, Hardy, and Yeats appealed only to a small, if discerning, public. But the novel flourished as never before. The great figures of the mid-Victorian era were passing from the scene. Thackeray and Dickens died before 1875, Trollope and George Eliot soon after. It had been an age when to be a great novelist was to be a best-seller. The *Cornhill Magazine*, launched in 1859, which regularly serialized these writers, had for many years a circulation of nearly 100,000 and, considering the size of Victorian families, must have reached at least half a million readers. The *Publishers' Circular* records the annual appearance of over a thousand new novels by 1890—nearly twice as many as twenty years earlier—but the best-sellers were no longer the best books. Hardy and Henry James were left far behind by Marie Corelli and 'Ouida'. There were however, plenty of minor masterpieces. A vintage year was 1894, which saw the publication of *Trilby*, *The Prisoner of Zenda*, *The Jungle Book*, and *The Diary of a Nobody*. P. G. Wodehouse, born in 1881, could have read them all as a schoolboy.

But the expansion and reform of education, the growth of a new reading public, and the increasing output of books from the publishers brought little benefit at first to the booksellers. The trade was in a bad way. It was suffering from a self-inflicted wound, the practice of underselling. '2d. in the 1/- DISCOUNT FOR CASH off New Books published at 2/6 and upwards' Blackwell announced on the cover of his first catalogue. Ten years later he was offering '3d. in the 1/-' for orders amounting to £3, though the discount he got from the publisher was normally no more than 4d. in the shilling, sometimes less. But no bookseller could expect to find buyers for new books at the full published price. It was a choice between selling none or selling with little or no profit. Books were 'nothing but appendages to toyshops and Berlin-wool warehouses' Alexander Macmillan[1] wrote to Gladstone in 1868. Until the Net Book Agreement came into force in 1900 it was only the second-hand books that paid their way. They had by then been the backbone of the trade (apart from toys and Berlin-wool—and patent medicines) for more than half a century. The increase in the output of new books, which rose from 4,904 in 1875 to 7,149 in 1900, did little good to booksellers—until they found their way into the second-hand market.

But, in the depressed condition of the trade in 1879, Blackwell had two great advantages. He had set up shop in a University town ('an educated man', Humphrey Milford[2] said, 'spends 10% of his income on books') and he was a true bookman, a lover of literature and bibliophile. 'Out round Headington Hill before breakfast, learning *Il Penseroso*' he wrote in his diary one day, and on another 'In Christ Church Meadows 6.30 [a.m. of course] reading *The Princess*'. He taught himself Latin, tackling Caesar's Gallic Wars with the help of Smith's *Principia Latina*. He memorized that catalogue of Bernard Quaritch. No wonder that the dons who came to see what the new shop was like soon became regular customers, among them Quiller-Couch of Trinity and the celebrated Master of Balliol, Benjamin Jowett. Dr Jowett bought a folio *Diodorus Siculus* (for

---

[1] Alexander Macmillan (1817–96), co-founder, with his elder brother Daniel (1813–57), of Macmillan's.

[2] Sir Humphrey (Sumner) Milford (1877–1952), man of letters and Publisher to the University of Oxford, 1913–45; originator of the *Oxford Dictionary of Quotations*.

7*s*. 6*d*.) in November 1879 and paid for it in March 1881, one of the earliest instances of the very popular fallacy that 'Blackwell's are in no hurry to be paid'. The fact was that the Oxford booksellers vied with each other in giving longer and longer credit to attract and retain customers, and who more valuable than the Head of a College? Moreover, if a customer paid cash he was entitled to the discount. Better wait, and get the full published price. But it was a most false economy, especially when applied to the junior members of the University. 'How few undergraduates', Sir Maurice Bowra remarked many years later, 'realize, when they leave Oxford, how much they owe to Blackwell's'.

III

The Business Comes of Age
1879–1900

THE young business got quickly into its stride, and in 1883 Blackwell felt enough confidence in its future to purchase the freehold of the whole of No. 50, and he and his mother moved from Holywell to live over the shop. This transaction was carried out partly with further help from Mrs Messer, who lent him £1,150 on mortgage at four per cent, partly by means of a loan from Barclays Bank, though Mr Parsons shook his head gravely and remarked that 'it is not banking to lend money on old houses'. Sales were now running at £3,000 a year, and were to rise to £15,000 before the end of the century. There was a corresponding increase in the amount of stock held—over 100,000 volumes by 1900—and room had to be found for this rising tide of literature, so in this same year, 1883, Blackwell acquired the lease of Lockwood the tailor's shop next door, at No. 51, at a rent of £40 a year. It was not long before the business began to overflow also into the patchwork of old buildings that lay between the Broad Street houses and the gardens of Trinity College. No. 2 Bliss Court was the first to be taken over and used for packing and housing reserve stock. Bliss Court, named after a former owner, not for its amenity, lay at the back of Nos. 48 and 49.

It deserves a memorial not only for its 'Continental' charm, shown in W. Russell's wood engraving, but for its interest to students of *forensic* medicine. It consisted of a row of cottages, with windows and doors on one side only, facing the wall of buildings across a passageway five or six feet wide. The wall was adorned with window boxes where hanging

BLISS COURT
Engraving by W. Russell

ferns throve best, for sunshine and healthy breezes rarely visited these blind cottages. There were three communal 'offices' at the end of the yard, and water was supplied by one standpipe in the middle distance. The cottages in my memory were occupied by poor and elderly widows, whose standard of health was exemplary. Everybody wanted them to go— the Medical Officer of Health, the Landlord, and the Bookshop, which flooded into each cottage as it fell vacant. There they lived on and on; but if any one of them had an accident and was removed to hospital, she died almost at once.[1]

But Benjamin Henry bore their longevity with kindly patience. His diary notes reveal a regular gift of money at Christmas for presents for them and for apples and oranges for the few children living in the buildings.

In the course of time other premises, hitherto occupied by such varied tenants as the Churchmen's Union and a boxing coach named Dolley, were acquired, and filled with books. Verlaine once came to give a lecture—to a very small audience—in the Dolley room, and had to thread his way through 'un dédale de chambres regorgeant de livres'. One of Blackwell's first apprentices, Fred Hanks, remembered how, as an inquisitive boy, he peeped through a crack and saw the poet addressing his select but intrepid audience by the light of two candles.

The series of Blackwell catalogues, preserved in the archives of the firm, provides good evidence for the way in which the business developed. There are seventy-two of them for the years 1879 to 1900, and their preparation, three or four a year, must have caused the founder to spend many hours of work on them outside shop hours. He taught himself to be a good bibliographer, but he tempered enthusiasm with modesty. At the end of the first catalogue appear some lines from Pynson's *Ship of Fools*:

> 'Styll am I besy bokes assemblynge, ...
> But what they mene do I nat understonde.'

Mindful of his critical University customers, he quoted at the head of catalogue No. 12 (May 1884) from the *Memoirs* of a great London

[1] Basil Blackwell.

bookseller, James Lackington, whose shop in Finsbury Square, 'The Temple of the Muses', had been one of the sights of London a century earlier: 'I contented myself', wrote Lackington, 'with reading the translations of the Classics, and inserted the originals in my catalogues as well as I could; and when sometimes I happened to put the genitive or dative case instead of the nominative or accusative, my customers kindly considered this as a venial fault, and bought the books notwithstanding.' In 1888 Blackwell produced a very select catalogue (No. 22), in which most of the hundred items were priced at more than £2. It was aimed at a discriminating public, and there appeared at the end, half apologetically, a passage from the *American Journal*: 'His [the cataloguer's] work has been so faithfully performed for him, a generation or two ago, by Brunet, Stevens, Lowndes, Dibdin, Allibone, Willis, Quaritch, and the rest of the old bibliographical guild, that all he has to do is to follow in their tracks and plagiarise at every footstep. . . . To compile a book catalogue in these days one only needs a paste-pot, a pair of scissors and a little horse-sense. That is the whole of the necessary equipment.'

Blackwell frequently cited the testimony of these authorities, and several others, to the merits of a book, but he added to the equipment listed by the *American Journal*, wide reading, a retentive memory, and a love of literature for its own sake, as is shown by the number and range of literary appreciations he quotes from Johnson, Hazlitt, Macaulay, Horace Walpole, Anthony Wood (for *Oxoniensia*), Isaac D'Israeli, and many others. Occasionally he allows himself a personal comment. 'Suckling was among the purest, if not *the* very purest, writer of his day that has gained any celebrity.' J. H. Burton's *The Book Hunter* is 'a delightful book'. Indignation shows itself in 'First edition of the Twenty-four Books (of Chapman's *Homer*). Some "Ishmaelite" has cut out the engraved title with scissors.'

Turnover of stock, the keystone of success in trade, seems to have been rapid from the outset. Barely a quarter of the books—all second-hand—listed in the January and April catalogues of 1879 reappeared in October, partly, perhaps, owing to the attraction of a new shop, partly also to the very low prices of some items. When

Catalogue No. 1 appeared Ingram Bywater, the future Regius Professor of Greek commemorated in R. W. Chapman's *Portrait of a Scholar*[1] is said to have left his breakfast untasted and hurried along Broad Street to secure a copy of Pacius' edition of Aristotle's *Organon* (1597) offered at 28*s*. Sometimes the books sold inconveniently fast, for the first apprentice, Fred Chaundy, remembered arranging books sideways in the shelves, to help fill up empty spaces.

But opportunities were not lacking in Oxford to replenish stock. Catalogues were soon appearing that included books 'scarce and valuable, chiefly purchased from Libraries recently dispersed'. Catalogue No. 16 (1886) had an 8-page section of over 300 volumes from the library of Mark Pattison,[2] which included a sumptuous group of early-printed editions of classical authors, a third of them from before 1600. The small quarto Junta *Sophocles* of 1522 was surely a bargain, even in those happy days, at 15*s*. Two years later an entire issue, headed '*Ex Oriente Lux*', was devoted to the library of the late Laudian Professor of Arabic, Robert Gandell, an erudite and polyglot assembly among which lurked, oddly, '*Robinson Crusoe*, Arabic text without woodcut illustrations, 2/-'.

In the same year Oliver Wendell Holmes received an honorary degree in the Sheldonian Theatre. Afterwards he visited the shop and Benjamin Henry noted in his diary:

a small figure came, none too nimbly, up the steps of the shop:

Dr H: Will you show me the book in the window, 'Rare Poems'?

BHB (producing book): This is really an American book.

Dr H (proudly): Well, and I'm an American.

BHB: Then I think I have the pleasure of speaking to Dr. Wendell Holmes, and of thanking him for the great pleasure I have gained from reading his book.

---

[1] Robert William Chapman (1881–1960), editor of Jane Austen and Samuel Johnson; Secretary to the Delegates of the Clarendon Press 1920–42.

[2] Mark Pattison (1813–84), Rector of Lincoln College, had amassed the largest private library in Oxford, some 14,000 volumes. They were sold at auction by Sotheby's in 1885, and it was no doubt at that sale that Blackwell bought his selection. Pattison was portrayed as Dr Casaubon in *Middlemarch*.

Dr H: Would you like an autograph? Bring me a copy of 'The Autocrat'.

Alas, there was none in stock! But among my own books is a highly valued copy of 'The Poet at the Breakfast Table' wherein the author's autograph appears. In bringing the Doctor a pen with which to write, it did not occur to me until he had gone down the steps that I should have regretted that it was not sapphire . . .

Another special catalogue of June 1894 is evidence not only of Blackwell's enterprise but of his standing in the University. In 1861 the Radcliffe Camera had been converted into a reading-room for the Bodleian Library, and Dr Radcliffe's 'Physic Library' of scientific books had been removed to the newly-built University Museum in Parks Road. It included, as it happened, some non-scientific books, and in 1893, to ease the pressure on the Museum shelves, the Radcliffe Trustees decided to sell such of these as were not wanted by the Bodleian. Blackwell bought them, nearly 800 volumes, some containing the bookplate of James Gibb, architect of the Radcliffe Camera.

At first the second-hand trade accounted for more than half Blackwell's sales, but the balance soon altered. Within five years the annual outlay on new books was beginning to exceed £1,000, and continued to rise rapidly. New books begin to appear in the Educational catalogues from 1887 onwards, side by side with second-hand, and in November 1894 a catalogue of new books for the general reader was issued, in time for Christmas. Visits to the bookshop opposite the Sheldonian Theatre were evidently becoming a family affair, for the catalogue contains a long section of books for children, and a still longer one of adult fiction, some 1500 titles. Among the children's books is a goodly muster of G. A. Henty's historical tales—forty-seven of them, and he was to write a dozen more before he died in 1902. Dozens, too, by R. M. Ballantyne, G. Manville Fenn, W. H. G. Kingston, and Jules Verne, and, for a more feminine taste, L. T. Meade (*A Sweet Girl Graduate* anticipated women's degrees at Oxford by more than thirty years), Mrs Marshall, and Mrs Molesworth. *Alice in Wonderland* is there but Peter Rabbit had not yet been born.

The adult fiction section contains, of course, the major novelists of the Victorian age, and earlier, with the notable exception of Trollope, whose popularity collapsed suddenly after his death in 1883. The younger generation appear, too, Hardy, Kipling, Meredith, Stevenson. Novelists of the second rank, and lower, are there in abundance: Lever, Lytton, Harrison Ainsworth, and F. Marion Crawford, 'Ouida', Marie Corelli, and Hall Caine, and some whose very names are forgotten. Who today remembers Amelia E. Barr, whose list of twenty-one books includes *Feet of Clay* (with author's portrait) and *Love for an Hour is Love for Ever*?

Poetry and Drama, Religion, History, and Biography, Natural History (fourteen books on British Ferns), Reference Books, Annuals and Almanacs (including, surprisingly, a *Football Annual*), all are there. Blackwell was by now catering for all tastes and all ages, from *Our Little Ones' Library* (done up in a case, with silk ribbon, 1s. 6d.) to the *Encyclopaedia Britannica* (24 vols.).

In 1888 he had been appointed by the Oxford Union Society to supply the foreign books for their library, and in 1895 his first catalogue of Foreign Books appeared, French, German, Italian, and Spanish. A note informed customers that 'B. H. Blackwell having agents in the leading Continental Cities is enabled to obtain Foreign Works, not in stock, with the utmost promptitude and at the lowest rates.' This was a considerable coup, for this business had hitherto been the exclusive preserve of Parker's. Blackwell was at pains to maintain his standing with his fellow tradesmen, particularly with the one among them still mightiest in influence in the city. 'I should like to ask, as a favour,' he wrote to the Librarian, 'that, if it be possible, Messrs Parker's may understand the change has not been the result of any application on my part, so that there may be no room for ill-feeling towards me.'

It is not only the widening range of the stock of books that the early catalogues demonstrate, but the way in which their sales were spreading beyond Oxford. 'The new Parcels Post', an 1883 catalogue points out (at 3d. for parcels not exceeding 1 lb. rising to 1s. for those not exceeding 7 lb.), 'affords great facilities for the despatch of books to all parts of the country.' Three years later appears the telegraphic address BLACKWELL BOOKSELLER OXFORD. The issue of an 'advance impression for America' of one of his 1896 catalogues shows that he had gained a footing in the export market in which the firm was to become so pre-eminently successful in the future.

But expansion could only come from a strong home base, and Blackwell's links with the University were becoming stronger every year. Nor was it only the books that drew people to the friendly shop where you could browse undisturbed by solicitous salesmen— a 'custom of the house' from the start. The Regius Professor of History, Bishop William Stubbs, who lived almost next door, in Kettell Hall, until 1884, is recorded as saying 'Mr. Blackwell's shop is the literary man's house-of-call.'[1] Young Mr Blackwell's enthusiasm and literary taste won him many friends and helped to mould the character of the business.

The undergraduate poets and scholars brought him their verses and their Prize Compositions to publish. In the very year that he set up shop his imprint appeared on a small book, *Mensae Secundae: Verses written in Balliol*, and in the following year he took over the publication of a terminal magazine of Oxford poetry, *Waifs and Strays*. It had a short life, but the contributors included James Rennell Rodd, J. St. Loe Strachey, H. C. Beeching, and J. W. Mackail, undergraduates of Balliol, and A. E. Housman of St. John's. It fore-shadowed the long series of volumes of *Oxford Poetry* launched by Basil Blackwell when he joined his father in 1913.

Beeching, 'the wisest and wittiest of my Balliol contemporaries' as one of his friends described him, became rector of Yattendon in 1885, and there collaborated with his neighbour Robert Bridges and H. E. Wooldridge in producing the *Yattendon Hymnal* (1895–9), which they brought to Blackwell to publish. It had an influence far outside the country parish for which it was first prepared—in par-ticular Vaughan Williams's *English Hymnal* owed much to it—and was the most distinguished book to bear the Blackwell imprint in

---

[1] 'house-of-call': The accurate, if old-fashioned, term for a place where men of the same calling congregate (Dickens uses it in *Martin Chuzzlewit*) was long ago changed to 'public house' in Blackwell family tradition.

the nineteenth century. Beeching, who became Dean of Norwich, remained a lifelong friend of the Blackwell family. Bridges became a frequent visitor to the shop in Broad Street after he had left Yattendon, twenty-five miles away beyond the Berkshire Downs, and moved into his new house on Boars Hill in 1907. He would stride along the Broad, his leonine head surmounted by an untidy broad-brimmed hat, a satchel over his shoulder to hold his purchases, to talk about men and books to the Founder, and in later years to his son. He once warned Basil not to leave the quiet paths of book-selling for the perilous course of publishing. 'Anybody can be a publisher but there is only one Blackwell's—and never alter the front of 50 and 51.' Bridges was a discerning and loyal friend but by no means hail-fellow-well-met.

One had to walk delicately. Once I addressed him as 'Doctor'—that was a mistake. I offered to shake hands when I found him in his garden the first time I visited him at his home on Boars Hill, and found that I was about to grasp the nipping end of a pair of secateurs; and once my undertaking on behalf of an unknown author to invite the Laureate to accept a copy of his book left me with a difficult letter to write. I have best cause to be grateful to him for making me understand my father's achievement.[1]

It was Mackail who started the custom of bringing Prize Compositions to be published by Blackwell. The winners recited their pieces, or passages from them, at the Encaenia in the Sheldonian Theatre, and printed copies had to be available on the day, near the end of June. The interval between award and recitation was sometimes uncomfortably short. 'Hudson Shaw's Stanhope printed at Clarendon Press' wrote Blackwell in his journal of 12 June 1882, 'got out of bed twice, 12.30 and 1.30 a.m., to take in proofs.' They had to be printed rapidly (and sometimes in 'unsocial hours') but they sold slowly, and although they were, with two exceptions, printed at the author's expense and published 'on commission', they can hardly have been profitable. In a catalogue of 1899 that lists the whole series—89 of them—only six are marked 'out of print'. Still, Black-

---

[1] Basil Blackwell.

well became in this way the first publisher of many who were to become famous in scholarship and literature, among them Gilbert Murray, Laurence Binyon, and John Buchan.

The esteem in which he was held by the young poets in the University is shown by the story of the Horace Club. Founded in 1898, this was a literary club with a difference. The members met, not to discuss other men's works, but to rehearse their own. Each was bound to produce, and read to his fellows, a poem written for the occasion 'in a well-known language' and 'not exceeding in length, nor falling below in brevity, any poem of Horace (excluding the *De Arte Poetica*)'. The ordinary members (still in residence as dons or undergraduates) included Raymond Asquith, Hilaire Belloc, John Buchan, A. D. Godley, St. John Lucas, and Arnold Ward (the club's founder, a greatnephew of Matthew Arnold), and the honorary members (no longer in residence), H. C. Beeching, Laurence Binyon, Meade Falkner, and W. R. Hardie (who invariably produced a poem in Greek) and two Cambridge men, Maurice Baring and Owen Seaman. The Keeper of the Records was B. H. Blackwell. When the club's sparkling but brief career ended in 1901 he published all the contributions in *The Book of the Horace Club*. The original albums—the 'Records'—in which the autograph poems were pasted after each meeting, survive, a moving monument to Victorian wit and scholarship.

Senior members of the University brought Blackwell lectures and pamphlets, which can hardly have earned their keep, though Professor Cook Wilson's Inaugural Lecture *On an Evolutionist Theory of Axioms*, which went into a second impression, sold better than his *Manual of Cyclist Drill for the Use of the Cyclist Section of the O.U.R.V.C.* There were commercially successful books as well. Most of these were for the use of undergraduates in preparing for examinations, but a few reached a more general public, only to be transferred subsequently to London publishers: Oman's *Art of War in the Middle Ages*, for example, to Longman and Warde Fowler's *A Year with the Birds* to Macmillan. It was not until young Basil joined his father in the firm in 1913 that publishing became more than a somewhat casual concomitant to bookselling.

IV

The Pillars of the House

'IF my father', said Sir Basil Blackwell at the firm's 75th-anniversary lunch in Christ Church Hall, 'had thought, in the first week of January 1879, to commemorate the founding of his firm by sitting at lunch with his staff, he would have sat down alone.' A year later he would have had company—one apprentice. On the firm's twenty-first birthday they would have been a party of about a dozen.

That first apprentice was F. W. Chaundy, who was once heard to say that he 'saw a good deal of Lewis Carroll at one time', and explained that when he called at his rooms in Christ Church to collect some books shortly after nine one morning, Mr Dodgson was still in his bedroom, whence he emerged clad only in his shirt. He turned his back, and stooped down to gather the books from the floor; his shirt was a 'cutty-sark', it had no tail. Fred Chaundy left Blackwell's when his apprenticeship was over and, after working for William George's Sons in Bristol, came back to Oxford as manager of a shop that George's had acquired in the High Street. Later, he bought this business from them—Blackwell with characteristic generosity lent him £100 to complete the deal—and carried it on as 'Chaundy's' until the early twenties, when he acquired the business of Dulau and Co. in London. He and his son Leslie put new life into this antiquarian bookshop, founded at the end of the eighteenth century and famous for its expertise in botanical books. In 1940 the entire premises and stock were destroyed by an enemy bomb and his son killed. 'In these tragic circumstances it seemed appropriate that Fred Chaundy should be invited to return to the firm in which he was apprenticed; so we acquired the goodwill of

Dulau and the good fortune of having Fred Chaundy under our roof.[1] He carried on business happily as the Dulau department of Blackwell's until his death in 1947, after sixty-seven years in the book trade.

Today young people go to their first job after several years of secondary education, and perhaps some more at a Technical College or a University. They have certificates and diplomas and degrees as evidence of their qualifications. Staff recruitment in the nineteenth century was quite a different matter, a matter, largely, of chance. Who could tell how a small boy with nothing but a few years of elementary education behind him would turn out? But Blackwell's boys certainly turned out well. Some of his early recruits were to spend the whole of their working lives in the firm, and their skilled and devoted service helped to lay the foundations of its developing prosperity.

SS Philip and James, those conjoint saints deplored by Charles Lamb for furnishing between them at their feast but one school holiday, may be regarded as the patron saints of Blackwell's; for in those early days they found for my father a succession of apprentices, of whom the first four were Fred Chaundy, Fred Hanks, Harry Chaundy, and Will Hunt. The brothers Chaundy, having served their time, left, as apprentices commonly did, to enlarge their experience in other bookshops, and both eventually became booksellers in their own right. Fred Hanks and Will Hunt stayed with the firm, Will Hunt until death took him in January, 1939, Fred Hanks until his retirement, in the sixty-fifth year of his service in 1948. These two, for many years my father's devoted lieutenants, and from 1919 his colleagues, and mine, were customarily called the 'Pillars of the House'; but they were more than that; pillars support a building, these were builders all their days. To me they were perfect colleagues, rejoicing in their work, utterly loyal to the firm, and proud that its fame and name should grow without thought of their own.[1]

Fred Chaundy reminded Sir Basil, many years later, of a practice which lasted until 1914. In the Long Vacation booksellers' second-hand stocks were cleaned by carrying the books out into the street, placing them on shutters set across boxes in the gutter, and banging

[1] Basil Blackwell.

them together to expel the dust. Volley and countervolley rever-
berated across the street, startling the horses in the hansom cab rank
in Broad Street and assailing the ears of the men who, at that season,
were busy weeding between the cobbles in the High.

By 1883, when the premises began to expand, the business could
carry another apprentice. 'Fredk. Hanks began to come today, on
trial as an apprentice' wrote Blackwell in his diary on 4 June. At his
binding, a month later, his mother said 'I hope he will be a good
boy.'

There is in the early life and circumstances of Fred Hanks a strong
similarity to those of my father.

I quote from what he told us at the *fête champêtre* in my village of
Appleton when we celebrated his Jubilee in 1933, and the conferment on
him of the Honorary Degree of MA by the University.

My father died when I was five years old, and my mother, who was
left penniless, literally became the breadwinner. The only education
she could afford to give me was that provided by the elementary schools
at 2*d.* a week. It must have been when I was about eight years old
that my mother, anxious to do all she could to supplement my elementary school education, thought it would be good for me to 'learn
a little French'. I remember accompanying her to a bookseller's shop,
where she purchased for me with her hard-earned pennies a French
grammar. This was, so far as I remember, the first book I ever possessed.

It was, in fact, the germ of Blackwell's Foreign Department, and it
came about thus. A year or two after the purchase of the French grammar
SS. Philip and James' Boys' School was opened and little Hanks became
one of the first pupils. A small Latin was taught there in its early days,
and he remembers gratefully the 'extramural' coaching he received from
the vicar in French and in Latin to the stage of Caesar's *Gallic Wars*,
Book I. As a boy in the Church choir Hanks's place was immediately
beneath my father, and with a proper regard for his appearance (and
perhaps inspired by the example of Aaron) he used to constrain his
rebellious hair by an unguent which assailed my father's nostrils with
something less than the savour of a sweet sacrifice. 'One Sunday morning
after Church Mr Blackwell spoke to me for the first time, and asked me
very nicely and kindly if I would mind not using this particular hair-

F. J. HANKS

lotion. The next Sunday I obediently turned up in my usual place with my hair in its natural and inoffensive state, and you can imagine my surprise when, after the service, Mr Blackwell spoke to me for the second time, thanking me very nicely and at the same time placing a shilling in my hand. In the course of time, hearing that Mr Blackwell required an apprentice I boldly applied, and on 1 July 1883 my indentures were signed, and there I am still in 1933.'

'F.J.H.' was there still in 1943 and for five years after that, and through-out those sixty-five years he 'put heart and soul' (his familiar phrase) into the business. It is of a piece with my wonderful good fortune through life in my friends and colleagues that I inherited this perfect loyalty; the hand that rocked my perambulator in the little garden behind 51 Broad Street was my right hand for nearly a quarter of a century after I became Chairman of B. H. Blackwell Ltd.[1]

Next, Will Hunt, apprenticed in 1889.

In the year of my birth, and in a happy hour, my father bound apprentice another SS Philip and James chorister. This was Will Hunt. 'Vigorous, straightforward, and conscientious' as F.J.H. described him, his honest and eager soul conceived at once and always held an admiring devotion to my father.

In youth, like his seniors, Will Hunt had an urge to learning, and as Latin and French were no longer taught at the Church school, Fred Hanks helped him in the rudiments after the day's work was done. But his star led him into the field of new English books, and his enthusiasm, accuracy, and exceptional gift of memory came to the service of the business at the apt hour. New Universities were being founded in the Provinces and the Empire (it was the Empire then) and Oxford men were helping to build them. These, remembering their happy hours in 50 and 51 Broad Street, sought from Blackwell's books for their teaching and for the nascent libraries. Will Hunt delighted in the work and applied to it the discipline of infinite pains which he had learnt from 'his said master'. He had that rarest of gifts in business of infallibly fulfilling any promise or undertaking. He never forgot. Over the years old Oxford men would return to thank him for his exact and punctual care for their needs and interests; they would be recognized and convincingly welcomed by this exemplary bookseller; and year by year the bookshop became known to

[1] Basil Blackwell.

W. HUNT

a widening circle of scholars overseas. My father implanted in his first disciples a veneration for scholarship and to the end of his career to serve the cause of learning was for Will Hunt a mission to be enthusiastically fulfilled, and a matter of extreme good fortune, and high privilege.[1]

Hunt was always determined to satisfy the customer. If a young assistant showed signs of giving up the search for the publisher of an apparently unknown book, Hunt would say 'If the customer knows the book, so must we. Find it.' even if this meant a visit to the Bodleian Library equipped with a reader's ticket.

One more of the early recruits who, with Hanks and Hunt, was to become a director of the firm in 1920, must be commemorated.

I have now to tell of the third member of the founding triumvirate, Charles Field. He was somewhat junior to the first two; I think I remember him first as a young clerk in the Counting House *circa* 1895 working under the original cashier Lambert, a sterling character in my father's opinion, and perhaps a kinsman, for my grandmother's maiden name was Lambert. He died after a crude operation for appendicitis in 1898, and Charles Field succeeded him in an office which had once been the bedroom over two cottages immediately behind 50 Broad Street. There he worked at a long sloping bench with two assistants and an office boy all equipped with steel pens (lodged behind the ear when not in use) with which they wrote all day copying in detail entries from long parchment-bound day-books into ledgers under the name of the customer concerned. All the details were transcribed again on to 'tub-sized' account forms which were sent out at the end of Term.

Charles Field had invincible faith in his debtors; it was part of his sweet nature. 'Oh, he'll come up' he would say when the time was ripe— and over-ripe—to pass an account into the hands of the professional extortioners. And how often he was right—as in the case of a Lord Chancellor[2] whose three-figure account had not been cleared since his college days—but not always.

There was a serenity in Charles Field apt to the patient labour of his

[1] Basil Blackwell.

[2] Frederick Edwin Smith, Earl of Birkenhead (1872–1930), Lord Chancellor 1919–22, High Steward of Oxford University 1922-30. Bought books 'by the yard' and had them sumptuously rebound, a practice that must have depressed rather than enhanced the value of many first editions.

pen and a simplicity in that to his honest vision and sense of duty difficulties presented themselves not as problems, but as occasions for making
the right decisions. So he welcomed innovations as the pen gave way to
the typewriter, and the typewriter to the accounting machine.[1]

The child is father of the man, and the 'good boys' whom chance
brought to Blackwell became good men in the course of nature. But
it was not mere natural growth that made them good Blackwellians.
That was a matter of training and example. The master *made* the
man. It was the founder who taught them to become good bookmen
and inspired their loyalty.

Geoffrey Barfoot, who was engaged in 1912 and in the course of
fifty-six years with the firm progressed from office boy to Director,
remembered the careful patience of 'Mr Benjamin Henry' in teaching the young entrants the smallest details of their work. When he
found the boy Barfoot adorning his penmanship in the postal ledger
with vainglorious flourishes, he sent for him and pointed out that such
flourishes were no improvement and, what was more, wasted time
and paper. 'You must never cut string', and he was shown how to
pack parcels for the stockroom in the right way, so that the string
could be easily untied to take out a book and then tied up again.
Another employee, in the earliest days of the business, remembered
seeing 'the Boss' busy at his desk in Broad Street after the shop was
closed, while Mrs Blackwell sat quietly untying knots in the string
which had come on the morning parcels from London. His un-
affected vigilance does not seem to have grown less with the years.
A young apprentice was 'squaring up' the books in the shelves one
morning and speeding up the operation by running the palms of his
hands along the wooden edges when a voice behind him warned
him against the risk of splinters, and he was shown the proper way
to do the job. It was B.H.B. himself, only a few months before his
death in 1924.

Aristotle called a good man four-square, *tetragonos*. 'Square' had
no undertone of mockery among honest men in days gone by.
Harry Blackwell was a square man, upright, disciplined, patient,
undemonstrative, dutiful. But let his son portray him.

[1] Basil Blackwell.

My father was somewhat above middle height, slim, well-proportioned, and nimble at need. He had married in his late thirties and was in his forty-first year when I was born in 1889 (twenty months after my sister), and his hair was already sable-silvered.

Throughout my boyhood and youth at home the morning was greeted by song; it was a signal that my father had emerged from his cold bath and was rubbing down; the song continued while he dressed, then there was silence; he was kneeling in prayer in his dressing room. I have been told, that at one time before his marriage, in accordance with Psalm 55, 'at noon-day would he pray, and that instantly'. This was his private discipline; he obtruded his religion on no-one and rarely spoke of it, but to one daily in contact with him it was evident that his rule of life was 'to do justly, and to love mercy, and to walk humbly with his God'. He was loyal to the Church of England, sang alto in the choir of 'Phil and Jim' for many years till he was called to the office of churchwarden of St. Mary Magdalen, and later was a supporter of the new Church of St. Andrews in North Oxford for the rest of his life.

Following his father and grandfather he was a scrupulous teetotaller, but would offer wine (pretty bad, I suspect) and spirits to his guests. He was accessible at all times, though normally he was silent and abstracted at meals.

A Liberal, 'dreadful radical' according to Tommy Case[1] of Corpus he endured patiently the political assaults of my mercurial mother—a true-blue of Norfolk farming stock.

He never swore, albeit he put considerable emphasis into an occasional 'Dash it!'. His speech was always moderate, spiced with whimsical comments or literary allusions. 'Three times I have asked you to pass the salt' cried my sister sharply at dinner. 'Thrice the brindled cat hath mewed' was the instant response. He showed me once his reply to a letter from the Chief Constable reminding him that his dog licence had not been renewed. It read 'Vide Richard III, Act V, Sc. 5, line 2'.[2] He would say occasionally, with a deprecating glance at his achievement, 'It has been said that a self-made man relieves his Creator of a great responsibility.' (I have not traced the source—if indeed there be one—of this aphorism.)

---

[1] Thomas Case (1844-1925), a famous Oxford character, who called himself a Palmerstonian liberal, but vigorously opposed everything new-fangled, from the admission of women to Einstein's theory of relativity; President of Corpus Christi College 1904-1925.

[2] 'The bloody dog is dead.'

My father had a sense of public duty and served on the committees of many praiseworthy societies. For some years he was a member of the City Council, and I remember how grieved he was when the Chairmanship of the Library Committee on political grounds was assumed by one of the Conservative majority.

He had a veneration for learning, of which he was deprived by the circumstances of his early days. He was, perhaps, a scholar *manqué*; he was as well read as a very busy life would permit, and delighted in the society of learned men. He had an antiquarian bias, being acquainted with the grammar of heraldry, and having learned to copy manuscript illuminations. An example of his achievement hangs before me in my room in Broad Street. How did he find time to train himself in this lovely work?

I used to watch my father as he sat in his chair reading in the evening, and ask myself: how is it this man, so quiet, so apparently reclusive, is so highly esteemed by his friends and fellow citizens? Has he really something of greatness? Then I would recall what an unknown supporter said of him in public when he was a Liberal candidate of the Oxford City Council: 'There is one who could stand on Carfax, and not a man in Oxford could throw a stone at him.' He was, I judge, 'a good man and did good things'.[1]

[1] Basil Blackwell.

V

Consolidation: 1900–1913

THE opening years of the new century brought a feeling of springtide, *commencement de siècle*. The wise but remote old Queen was succeeded by a genial and popular King. The calamitous Boer War came to an end at last, and the defender of Mafeking founded the Boy Scout Movement. The Education Act of 1902 heralded rapid advances in education. Five new universities— Birmingham, Liverpool, Leeds, Sheffield, and Bristol—received their charters, and the Workers' Educational Association was founded. Popular newspapers, the *Daily Mail* (launched in 1896), *Daily Express* (1900), and *Daily Mirror* (1903) achieved circulations beyond the dreams of Victorian proprietors, and average readers were becoming more educated. The output of new books had doubled by 1914. Most important for booksellers, the publishers' Net Book Agreement came into force on New Year's Day, 1900, and at last the underselling that had for so long bedevilled the trade was to be brought under control.

The accounts of the firm show, however, that the founder had, at first, small cause for complacency. Though sales were fairly steady, and began to move up again in 1903, profits fell sharply and did not recover until 1905. But by 1913 the business was on a firm footing. Sales were over £27,000 (compared with £15,000 in 1901), and net profits were averaging 11 per cent of sales, before any drawings by the proprietor. The balance sheet gave a figure of £20,000 for capital, half of it stock in trade.

Blackwell decided that the time had now come to give his staff a share in the firm's growing prosperity. A profit-sharing scheme was drawn up in 1913 which provided that, after allotting a 'dividend' of 5 per cent on the capital to the proprietor, one-quarter of the remaining net profit should be awarded to the staff. There were then seventeen on the payroll (no women yet), of whom thirteen were to receive a bonus of $7\frac{1}{2}$ per cent of their wages, which ranged from £3 a week to 16s. for the most junior, the boy Smith. The remainder was divided, in varying proportions, between the four senior assistants, Hanks, Hunt, and Field, and Basil Blackwell, who had just joined his father. The decision was wise as well as generous. A warm and practical concern for 'Blackwellians' has been a notable feature throughout the firm's history, and long and faithful service has been the result.

In 1900 there was no early-closing day. Six (full) days a week did they labour and do all that they had to do, though perhaps not quite so much during the vacations, for Oxford was still predominantly a university town. When young Master Harold Macmillan came to Summerfields as a schoolboy in 1903 the only industries seemed to be printing and marmalade, 'both somehow appropriate'. Harry Blackwell remembered a bookseller who, in the vacations, spent much of his time playing chess with his assistant and somewhat resented the intrusion of a rare customer. But times were changing. In April 1910 thirty booksellers' assistants put their heads together and appointed five of their number, one of them Fred Hanks, to petition the Oxford branch of the Associated Booksellers (all proprietors) for a five-and-a-half day week. Their petition failed because, in the words of the branch's minute book, it was 'absolutely impossible to get a unanimous feeling in the Oxford book trade to close early on Thursday, either in vacation or term'. But they had not long to wait. In a 1912 catalogue correspondents are asked to 'note that, under the Shops Act (of 1911), business is suspended on Thursdays at 1 p.m.'

One of those who was awarded the $7\frac{1}{2}$ per cent bonus in 1913 was Herbert Steele, of whom Sir Basil writes:

In 1902 my father introduced a revolutionary device. It was a Hammond typewriter, a most ingenious machine which enabled its operator to type in various languages with appropriate letter forms, and with this instrument he introduced H. C. ('Bert') Steele, a short, stocky, red-haired youth, adept in the mystery of stenography.

Hitherto letters were hand-written, mostly, I believe, by my father in his graceful and exact script. Bert Steele pluralized as my father's secretary and Will Hunt's assistant; so he had a double training in bookselling and business method, which his alert mind absorbed and applied greatly to the benefit of the firm. Presently he became responsible for the supply of books ordered by customers in person or by ever growing post, and also gave special attention to binding orders in the days when school and college prizes, calf-bound and armed, were in regular demand.

As the years passed, his daily handling of books (delivered, many of them, by their publishers, *mirabile dictu*, within forty-eight hours of their ordering) furnished his memory with an inexhaustible store of titles, authors, their publishers, and, in those stable days, their price.

Abrupt in speech, short-tempered, but with no grudge, and subject to a little sly teasing by his juniors he was devoted to the firm, delighting in a regular task most competently performed.[1]

The 'sly teasing' is referred to more than once in the reminiscences written by members of the 'Old Guard', at Basil Blackwell's suggestion, and preserved in the archives. They provide a lively source of information about the men (and women) of the old days and what went on behind the scenes. On the ground floors of 50 and 51 stood the quiet rows of books, shelf above shelf, floor to ceiling, second-hand and new, folios and quartos and octavos, in cloth and leather; quiet, and sober, for picture jackets were hardly known before the 1914–18 war. Blackwell's looked like a library, not an emporium of loudly self-advertising wares. But behind these urbane rooms and corridors and corners where the flocks of customers browsed undisturbed—behind and above and underground—was another world of bustle and movement, and high spirits. There were always two or three apprentices about the place, and the common or garden boy, what Walter Bagehot called this 'small apple-eating animal', is not easily repressed. The boys in Broad Street had a healthy respect for their masters but cheerfulness was always breaking in. The 'sly teasing' of Bert Steele took the form of sprinkling sugar on the floor of his office. 'He would shuffle about and scrape his feet with annoyance, and threaten to kick the arse of the boy responsible.' There was

[1] Basil Blackwell.

some real, if clandestine, apple-eating too. Outside the windows of
the office (on the first floor) was 'an ancient apple-tree, reputed to
have been planted on the site of a cesspit. The apples, which owed
something to breeding or feeding, were of a magnificent flavour, as
I can testify, having speared many a one from the window with a
knife tied on the end of an umbrella. A little to the right stood two
pear trees against the old Union building.[1] The fruit was hard and
never much sought after.'

The Blackwell catalogues again provide evidence of the nature
of the business during the Edwardian era. It was a period of growth
and consolidation rather than innovation. The accounts tell us that
sales of new books increased faster than those of second-hand—by
1913 they were nearly three-quarters of home sales—but the second-
hand side flourished too, and was promoted with more energy than
ever. From 1906 to 1908 second-hand catalogues were issued
monthly except during the long vacations, and to an ever expanding
circle of customers, private and institutional, at home and abroad.
Many important libraries were bought, much the largest that of
York Powell, Regius Professor of Modern History from 1894 until
his death in 1904. The 3774 items filled three special catalogues.

Antiquarian books were becoming more expensive, but it was
still possible at the end of the period to buy a fine copy of Acker-
mann's *University of Oxford* for 12 guineas. The market price today
is about £500. One of the founder's leading interests was in books
on the fine and applied arts, and in a 1912 catalogue devoted to
them he advertised reproductions of the great masters in the recently
revived series of *Arundel Prints* and the new series of *Medici Prints.*
A note on one of the latter (a Filippo Lippi *Madonna and Child*)
stated that 'the original of the Virgin of this picture is said to be a
lady who inspired the artist with a romantic passion'.

As for new publications, their overall number, as we have seen,
more than doubled during the period. The greatest expansion took
place in the fields of science and medicine, economics and technology, but it was, too, a golden age for fiction, in quality and quantity,
and at all levels. *Nostromo*, *Mr. Polly* and *Zuleika Dobson*, *The Scarlet*

[1] The old abandoned building of the Churchmen's Union.

Pimpernel and *The Four Just Men*, *Peter Rabbit* and *The Wind in the Willows* all appeared between 1901 and 1911. It was also an era of cheap editions (though not yet paperbacks). The growing popular demand for 'serious' books ensured the success of two famous series, the *World's Classics* (1901) and *Everyman's Library* (1906). J. M. Dent made publishing history with the latter, of which fifty volumes appeared in its first year, the same year in which the *Loeb Series* of Greek and Latin authors with parallel English translations was launched. Dent aimed at the educational as well as the general market. Many years later, when the thousandth *Everyman* appeared, a competition in a Sunday newspaper to guess the best sellers in the series revealed that *David Copperfield* came top, but the runner-up was an abridgement in one volume of Sir William Smith's dictionaries of classical antiquities, biographies, and mythology.

As more and more space was needed to display this rising flood of new books it became more and more difficult to leave room for the customers, but Blackwell was determined to preserve the amenities of what the *Oxford Magazine* called his 'comfortable *taberna*'. In 1907 he circulated with his catalogues a leaflet calling attention to alterations at 50 and 51 Broad Street. 'A furnished room has been opened, upstairs, which may be found convenient by visitors wishing to examine books, write a note, or look through the literary papers; and may in some degree supply that lack of seating accommodation which, it is feared, ladies have sometimes found noticeable.'

The overseas market grew steadily in importance, and by 1913 accounted for 12 per cent of Blackwell's sales. Two leaflets sent out as early as 1902 and 1903 must have been aimed at American University libraries. One offered 542 mid-seventeenth-century tracts, quarto leather-bound, relating to the Civil War and the Commonwealth, for $350, and the other a complete set of the *Philosophical Transactions of the Royal Society* from 1665 to 1898 for $900. But India was far and away Blackwell's largest overseas market. Benjamin Henry built up this trade by cultivating the needs of the Indian Civil Service probationers studying in Oxford, for whose special requirements the University had built the nearby Indian Institute, opened in 1884 at the end of Broad Street. He soon outdistanced all competitors and virtually monopolized the supply of books to libraries and officials in India. The Indian mail's arrival, by P & O, on Monday mornings created a minor frenzy in Broad Street every week. Books not in stock had to be ordered that same day from the publishers, who supplied by return as a matter of course (happy days!), and the books were ready punctually to despatch on Thursday.

In 1903 the first Rhodes scholars arrived in Oxford and were to have an important effect on export sales, especially, at first, in South Africa. Rhodes University in Grahamstown was founded in 1904, and the librarian's first thought was to write to Blackwell's, which he had known as an undergraduate, asking if the firm could supply the needs of his library. Benjamin Henry wrote back to say he would be delighted to see to it, and at the librarian's request the spine of each book was blocked with the words 'Rhodes University Library' before it left Oxford. The practice was discontinued after the Second World War for the sake of economy, but when the Founder's great-grandson Miles visited the library in 1971 he was shown, in the stacks, the large number of titles with the old special lettering on the spine.

Other universities in Africa followed Rhodes' lead, and in time similar connections were made in Canada, New Zealand, and the USA. The sales were at first very small: Blackwell's charges to the University of British Columbia in March 1918 amounted to $4.02. 'For decades', writes Clifford Collins of the University of Canterbury, New Zealand, 'Blackwell's would hardly have covered their printing and postage costs by this business. For our part, we felt embarrassed at our meagre purchases, but the firm's policy turned out to be a good long-term investment.' It did indeed.

Blackwell had earned the reputation of being one of the most knowledgeable booksellers of his day, and became President of the International Association of Antiquarian Booksellers, founded in 1906, with a membership of fifty in Great Britain and twelve overseas, five of them in America. He had also been a founding member, in 1899, of the Oxford and District branch of the Associated Booksellers of Great Britain and Ireland serving in turn as secretary and chairman, and he was soon elected to the Council of the national body. The *ABGBI* was founded in 1895 with the express object of putting an end to the old devil of underselling. Old indeed, for the earliest attempt to end it had been made nearly sixty years before Blackwell opened his shop. The London booksellers had tried in 1812 to form an association of their own to ban underselling, but it had come to nothing. A self-appointed committee set up in 1829 was partially effective for a time, but there were many dissentient members in the trade, and in 1852 the conflict came out into the open. The committee's attempts at retail price maintenance were attacked by *The Times* as 'this anomalous interference with the free course of competition and the natural operations of trade'. The matter was referred to arbitration, the verdict went against the committee, and they 'retired hurt'. But the campaign was not over. A few publishers began to issue new books at 'net' prices, and to refuse to deal further with any bookseller who sold these at a discount. Even authors joined in the fight. Lewis Carroll insisted that Macmillan's should supply his books to the trade at a discount of not more than 2*d.* in the shilling, so as to leave no margin for underselling. It was, in fact, Frederick Macmillan, one of the second generation of the founding family, who brought matters to a head. In 1890 he published sixteen books at net prices, among them one with a challenging title, Alfred Marshall's *Principles of Economics.* At the same time he wrote to *The Times* deploring the disastrous effects on the book trade of underselling. 'I have no doubt that with the hearty co-operation of the retail trade the *net* system could be introduced'. The battle was on again, and this time the reformers were to win. The booksellers formed their association in 1895, the publishers followed suit a few months later, and after five years of co-operative effort the Net Book Agreement, the 'charter of the book trade', was signed in 1900. It was not challenged again until 1962, when it came before the Restrictive Practices Court, and was adjudged in the public interest.

The Booksellers' Association held its annual meeting at Oxford in 1906, and good progress was reported. Since 1900 the proportion of new books published net had risen from less than one-half to over 80 per cent. The *Publishers' Circular* of 14 July 1906 contains a long and cheerful account of this meeting, which had been organized by an Oxford committee of which Blackwell was the 'indefatigable hon. secretary'. Several publishers, among them J. M. Dent, Gerald Duckworth, Henry Frowde,[1] and William Heinemann, were guests at the dinner in Wadham College Hall, at which Blackwell, proposing 'Success to the Publishers' Association', made the speech of the evening.

He was, of course, by way of being a publisher himself. The list of his publications grew steadily during the Edwardian period, and by 1913 contained over 400 titles. But they were still, for the most part, the kind of local and ephemeral publications described in a previous chapter. They were bringing goodwill to the business, but little direct profit—an average of less than £200 a year—though many of the authors became famous when they sailed into the main stream of publishing in London. The founder wanted something more creative and positive. He had not the time to plan and carry out an active publishing policy himself, and perhaps felt that he had not the right qualifications for the task. His son should try his hand at it.

[1] Head of the London Office of the University Press and, since 1883, Publisher to the University of Oxford.

VI

Father and Son: 1913–1924

BASIL BLACKWELL was now in his twenty-fourth year, his father forty years older. Benjamin Henry had waited until he was satisfied that his business was securely established before he felt justified in embarking, 'discreetly, advisedly, soberly', on matrimony. In 1883 he met Lydia (Lilla) Taylor, whose sister, Charlotte, was the wife of an Oxford friend of his. They soon came to an understanding, but Lilla, too, put duty first. She was a farmer's daughter from Blo Norton in Norfolk. Her father, John Taylor, had prospered until he was ruined, and many like him, by the grim agricultural depression of the seventies, caused by the influx of cheap grain from the North American prairies and intensified by a long run of very bad winters. 'He sat at his bedroom window to watch his horses and possessions all being sold in the farm yard. Then he died, as so often happens, unrewarded for a good strong life', writes Mrs Dorothy Sumner Austin, Lilla's daughter and Basil's sister. Lilla, the last of the five Taylor daughters left at home, determined to devote herself to her old mother. 'By becoming the village schoolmistress and playing the harmonium in church she was able to keep her mother in the old farm until she died.' So it was that Lilla and Harry waited until 1886 to get married. They were both in their late thirties. 'I have no ambition, even if I had the chance, to make what's called "a fortune"', he wrote to her. 'If I can live comfortably and quietly, paying my way and bearing in mind the rainy days that must come, I shall I think be content, and in this I am sure you can and will help me. I think very little of mere wealth, and not much of mere birth, but rank far above both the riches of a well-stored mind and my ambition lies more in that direction,

BASIL BLACKWELL, 1925

with very little chance of being satisfied for simple want of time and several necessary qualities conspicuous by their absence.'

They started their married life 'over the shop' in Broad Street, and there their two children were born, Dorothy in 1887, Basil Henry on 29 May 1889.

I was born on the second floor, front. The view from the window has not changed, except for the erection of an electric-light standard. Broad Street was cobbled, as Merton Street is today, and very noisy, as the iron tyres and iron-shod hooves made a great clatter. The most exciting noise, however, was the sound of the band leading a circus procession, which made a tour of the inner part of the city regularly by way of advertising itself, and we rushed from the dining-room across the stairhead to the drawing-room (which is now my office), and stood on a chair to watch the procession go by: first, the band in a wagon drawn by two horses, followed by outriders on horseback in picturesque oriental costumes, then one or two cages of animals and sometimes an elephant, and then the triumphal coach showing Britannia on the top of a pyramid with accompanying nymphs below. Marriott House (53 Broad Street) in those days was occupied by Trinity undergraduates, and as Britannia passed in triumph a kind of snowstorm of sugar knobs came out of the window, from which Britannia's shield was able to protect her for the most part.[1]

Basil spent the first seven years of his life in the Broad Street house. 'Up the stairs came the blended scent of printer's ink, binder's paste, leather boards, and book-dust, which was destined to be the breath of my nostrils through life.' There was still a small garden at the back of No. 51 where the infant Basil's pram could be parked. Fred Hanks regarded it as part of his duties to report any urgent noises from that quarter. The shop itself was out of bounds to the children on work days, but a great place for hide and seek on Sunday, the only day when their father was not constantly at work, 'a kindly but reticent being, whose thoughts were elsewhere'. Companionship and diversion came from their high-spirited mother, whom her son remembers as still having something of the country air about her and who found it 'difficult to adjust herself to the stratified society of Victorian Oxford, being intolerant of the gulf between Towns-

[1] Basil Blackwell.

H. G. Gadney H. W. Chaundy F. J. Hanks J. Ayres W. Hunt W. G. Grant
A. Jeffs

THE QUADRACYCLE

folk and Gownsfolk, rather to the dismay of my father, who had
grown up to regard it as untraversible and fixed'. They were never
tired of listening to her country tales of life on the Norfolk farm.
One rare and special treat is remembered by Basil. His father had
learned to ride a bicycle—a penny farthing—in 1882. Fred Hanks
rode one too, but these machines were no use for purely business
purposes. 'Presently there was to be an ingenious tandem quadracycle, steered by the back rider while the front rider maintained his
balance by holding two bars which came up from a fixed point
behind him to the level of his saddle. On this machine (with a bundle
of book sacks lashed to the frame) master and man would make
journeys to buy libraries in the neighbourhood, leaving the bags

packed for collection and transport by railway or carrier's van.' It was on this trade vehicle, in a small basket-chair mounted in front, that Dorothy and Basil, one at a time, first tasted the pleasures of speed on the road.

By 1896 the family—and the books—needed more room. They moved out to North Oxford, half-way to Summertown, where new houses were going up along Linton Road, mostly for married dons. Ten years later the neo-Norman St. Andrew's Church was built there, and Benjamin Henry became one of the churchwardens. The Blackwells' house, No. 1, with its seven bedrooms, must have seemed very spacious after the upper floor of 51 Broad Street, but by no means extravagant. In those days nobody thought it remarkable, or imprudent, that a man who had been in business only seventeen years, with a staff of twelve and profits that had never yet exceeded £2,500 a year, should buy and live in a house of that size. Building costs, at less than 8*d.* a cubic foot, were little more than one-fiftieth of those in 1978, domestic servants (the Blackwells had two) were paid about 10*s.* a week—a housemaid rather less, a cook rather more—and coal was £1 a ton. The Blackwells were well-off but not rich.

It was now time that Basil ('he has had seven years' holiday' said his father) went to school. He began at a dame-school for about 40 boys kept by the Misses Mardon (Wilhelmina and Sarah),[1] and at 12, like most Mardonians, proceeded to Magdalen College School—John Johnson, later Printer to the University, was his senior there by a few years. Thence, in 1907, to Merton College with a post-mastership (Mertonese for scholarship), where he spent four busy and happy years, following the 'grand, old, fortifying, classical curriculum', rowing and playing rugger for his college. One of his contemporaries was Adrian Mott, who was to become his partner in publishing.

Blackwell senior, having made sure that his son should have the full education that he himself had missed, thought it well that he

---

[1] Stella Welford, the granddaughter of Edith Arnett, who taught at the school, has, for the last fifteen years been on the staff of Basil Blackwell Publishers.

should learn something of the mysteries of publishing before joining the firm. He had many friends among the publishers, one of them Henry Frowde. Blackwell must have talked to him about his plans for his son—perhaps at the Booksellers' Association dinner in Wadham in 1906—for, when Basil was nearing the end of his time at Merton, Frowde suggested that he might spend a year (it turned into sixteen months) with the Oxford University Press in London 'to gain some insight into publishing', and to Amen Corner he went in September 1911.

There was no formal course of training. He was left to find his way about, and he was given a job to do. This was to complete the selection of *A Book of English Essays* (three parts done by Stanley Makower before his death) for the *World's Classics*, and see it through the press. His name thus appeared on a title page for the first time, as joint editor. Amen Corner gave him a practical, if unsystematic, introduction to publishing, and one for which he never ceased to be grateful. It is to be hoped that the inclusion, in the programme of the Associated Booksellers' dinner at Oxford in 1913, of a recitation (by Mr Charles Cruickshank) entitled 'Trouble at Amen Corner' had nothing more than a jocular significance. Many years later, on his eightieth birthday, Basil was entertained to lunch by Colin Roberts, then Secretary to the Delegates of the Clarendon Press, and presented with a Sheffield plate coffee-pot formerly used by Henry Frowde.

On New Year's Day 1913, then, Basil, back in Oxford, joined his father in Broad Street, and in September the Publications Department began a separate existence. Within two years came the war. For some years the nations of Europe had, in A. J. P. Taylor's memorable phrase, 'faced each other in a pre-war spirit'. The prospect of foreign invaders on British soil was viewed by the public with a patriotic mixture of suspicion and indignation, and the theme was a favourite one with authors. Erskine Childers's *Riddle of the Sands* (1903) was one of the earliest, and best, of the novels. A melodrama, *An Englishman's Home*, thrilled London audiences in 1909 with the spectacle of the brave civilian defending his 'castle' against the vile foreigner. At the annual Crystal Palace firework display the show ended with a stirring, noisy, and most enjoyable set-piece representing the British Army driving the baffled foe from a corner of the homeland. The theme became so popular that it attracted ridicule. P. G. Wodehouse, still under 30, wrote *The Swoop! Or How Clarence Saved England*—Clarence was a Boy Scout—and Harry Graham's *Ruthless Rhymes* included the lines 'I was playing golf the day the Germans landed, . . . And the thought of England's shame Altogether spoiled my game.' Like many of his contemporaries Basil had joined the Oxford University Officers' Training Corps as an undergraduate—T. E. Lawrence was one of those who trained with him in the Signals Section. He expected, therefore, to go straight into the army when war broke out, but the medical board decided that his eyesight was not good enough, and indeed on the rifle range he had never succeeded in hitting the target. He was to remain at his desk in Broad Street.

The war so long expected took many by surprise when it did come. An International Exhibition of Books and Graphic Arts was being held that summer in Leipzig, then the centre of the German industry, and the British Pavilion, housing an impressive array of the publishers' products, had to be hastily closed. The first separate catalogue of Blackwell's publications department, with a hopeful 'new look'—varied type, extracts from reviews, and some illustrations—was destined to make its appearance in September.

'Business as Usual' announced the nation of shopkeepers, but with rapidly diminishing conviction. There are no reliable statistics for the trade as a whole in those individualistic days, but many booksellers were certainly hard hit. Blackwell's sales went down by more than one-third and profits were halved. Second-hand books suffered most. Their sales had reached nearly £7,000 in 1913. By 1916 they had dropped to less than £3,000. The undergraduates who came up after the war, in 1919, were the gainers. They found Blackwell's shelves full of the books they needed. You could, for example, buy— a 1919 catalogue confirms the memory—a copy of the Oxford text of Thucydides, interleaved and bound in buckram, for 7s.

Two Blackwellians lost their lives in that war, Harris and Pinkney, promising young apprentices. The other serving members including

Bert Steele, a future director, returned to a business that quickly recovered in the short-lived post-war boom. By 1920 profits were running at the rate of £7,000 a year, more than double the pre-war level. In that year the firm was incorporated as a private limited company, and the first directors' meeting was held on 22 March. The founder was Chairman and his five fellow-directors were his son, the three 'pillars of the house' Hanks, Hunt and Charles Field, and H. S. Critchley, who was appointed Secretary of the company.

Harry Critchley, after completing his training as a chartered accountant in Bristol, had come to Oxford in 1906 and set up his brass plate at 5–6 Magdalen Street, over the Penny Bazaar. 'Since he and the office boy had nothing to do', writes his son John, 'they both used to rush to the window whenever a car passed by. Would it were the same now!' A year later his diary (25 March 1907) records 'Mr. B. H. Blackwell called 12.45, interview re posting books.' In the following week he began his duties, going at first almost every day for two or three hours to Broad Street. His charges for his first year's work, 184 hours, came to £23. 12s. 'When I returned from my happy experience at the OUP, Amen Corner', writes Sir Basil, 'I found that at noon, when my father left his room for his mid-day rest and refreshment at his home in North Oxford, Harry Critchley used to come in and "write up" certain account books. My room was adjoining, and the party door being open we enjoyed a desultory conversation concerning business matters, local affairs, and affairs of the world in general. He was eight years older and richer in worldly experience and wisdom, and he taught me much of men and manners in commerce. He had my father's entire confidence and mine, and to the end of his life I regarded him as my business father-confessor.' Critchley's colleague R. J. Pigott was appointed auditor to the new company, and thus began an association with the firm of Critchley, Ward and Pigott that has lasted to the present day.

The original share capital of B. H. Blackwell Ltd. was £25,000, divided into 7,000 7% cumulative preference shares allotted to the Chairman and 18,000 ordinary shares, of which 14,025 were issued. The assets were 'all the property capable of manual delivery', and the

THE UNION ROOM, 1920

Note the gaslight

amount owed to the firm by the credit customers, about £20,000. The premises in Broad Street remained the property of the Chairman, and the company paid him a modest rent. Father and son held the majority of the ordinary shares, 2,200 were allotted in various proportions to the other four directors, and 100 each to the other founding members of the company, H. Steele, W. Bates, H. S. Rowles, H. Cook, B. Presley, and C. W. F. Bishop. The profit-sharing scheme introduced in 1913 was discontinued, but other employees were selected to become shareholders year by year, and in 1923 a pension scheme was introduced. This provided, through endowment insurance policies, an income of 30s. a week at age 65, the cost of the premiums being borne equally by the staff and the company.

The numbers employed in the business after the war rose from 32 in 1919 to 45 in 1924. The accounts for the year ending 31 August 1924 show a total expenditure of some £6,000 on salaries and wages. Most of the recruits to the staff still came as apprentices, straight from school, undertaking, as Blackwell's first apprentice, F. W. Chaundy, had in 1880, to serve faithfully for five years, not 'to waste the Goods of his said Master . . . not contract Matrimony within the said Term nor play at Cards or Dice Tables . . . haunt Taverns or Playhouses'. The boy Chaundy started to learn 'the Art of a Bookseller' at 3s. 6d. a week, rising to 10s. in the fifth year. Forty years later the rate was 7s. 6d. rising to 20s. Thereafter the normal annual increment was 5s. a week, which meant serving twelve years more before reaching £4 a week. Apart from the Directors, William King (later head of the Antiquarian Department, whose career is commemorated in Chapter XIII) seems to have been the highest-paid member of the staff in 1924. He was then a married man of 32 with two children, and his salary had just gone up to £4. 7s. 6d.

Booksellers' assistants were not well paid in those days, though Blackwell's wages were above the provincial average. But most people were better off than before the war. By 1922 the cost of living had settled down to about twice the pre-war level but average wages were three times as high. Everybody walked or cycled to work (as they did for the next 25 years) and there were no expensive gadgets—no washing machines, no TV—to swell the household budget. A three-bedroom house could be built for £500. Few undergraduates in Oxford paid more than £3 a week for their digs, all meals included. Prices were not only lower in relation to earnings, they were also stationary. When a customer asked you the price of a book you could be sure that it hadn't just changed—and that it wouldn't. Everyman's Library (of which, in the twenties, Blackwell's reckoned to sell a volume every twenty minutes) was now 2s. and there it would stay (until the next war). 'Inflation' was a word used only, by the ordinary man, in connection with balloons.

Shopkeepers in general, and booksellers in particular, still worked long hours. Apart from the introduction of the five-and-a-half day week in 1911, there had been little change since Harry Blackwell began his apprenticeship to the trade fifty years earlier. In Broad Street work began at 8.30 and, except on early-closing day, the shop kept open during term until 8.0 p.m., and in the first and last weeks until 9.0 p.m. With an hour off for lunch and another hour for tea the normal term-time working week was 52 hours, and 57 hours at beginning and end. Work was not always over when the shop closed—'the day's work must be finished in the day'—and there was no such thing as higher payment—*any* payment indeed—for over-time. But out of term the shop closed at 6 p.m., and everyone had a fortnight's holiday in the Long Vacation.

At the first Annual General Meeting of the new Company, on 13 December 1920, the Chairman was able to report that the results of the past year's working had been 'unexpectedly successful . . .' He could not promise 'that the ensuing year would be as successful, but as Oxford was not a manufacturing town a depression in trade was not so likely to occur'. Six months later car production at the Cowley works (William Morris had put up his first modest building there in 1919) was to soar to 350 a month, and the industrialization of Oxford had begun. But Blackwell's first delivery van, bought for £281 in 1921, was a Chevrolet.

The Chairman's forecast was a good one. Profits fell slightly in the company's second year, but they rose in 1922 to £8,429—the highest yet—and the dividend on the ordinary shares was raised from 15 per cent to 17½ per cent. Then came two years in which, though sales increased, expenses increased more, and profit slipped below £8,000 again. The business 'seemed to be marking time'.

The founder was in his seventieth year when the company was formed, and was to be Chairman for less than five years. In March 1922 'my father', writes Sir Basil, 'had the misfortune of a fall from his bicycle in collision with a taxicab, causing a concussion which would have been more severe but for the strong brim of his bowler hat. I watched with dismay the decline of his vigour, his withdrawal from public life. He retired from the City Council and felt bound to decline the Presidency of the Booksellers' Association, of which he had been a founding member. His mind showed signs of fatigue and a reluctance to entertain new projects.' On 26 October 1924 he died at his home in Linton Road after a short illness, aged 75.

He had set up shop in a room so small that there was barely space for one customer and one chair. He had watched the business grow in 45 years into one of the best-known bookshops in the world. Its future was in safe hands. His son was ready to succeed him as Chairman, with an experienced and loyal staff to support him. There was already a grandson, six-year-old Richard, who might perhaps turn out well. In the event, Basil was to rule as Chairman of the firm for exactly the same period as his father, 45 years, and was to be succeeded by that same Richard.

'Mr. Blackwell lived a quiet life—he had no clubs and no cronies. His whole life and interest were in his business' wrote the obituarist in the *Oxford Chronicle* in a long and warm tribute to this great citizen. Cronies and clubs he may not have had, and he lived for his business, but he made many friends and found time for many public duties. He was a 'character', and seems to have drawn men to him by a certain mixture, an irresistible mixture, of charm and rigour and integrity. One of his earliest customers, and oldest friends, Sir Michael Sadler,[1] who came up to Trinity in 1880, the year after Blackwell opened his shop, wrote to Basil in 1938 'Your

[1] Sir Michael (Ernest) Sadler (1861–1943), educational pioneer, Vice-Chancellor of Leeds University, 1911–23, Master of University College, Oxford, 1923–34.

father's untiring, friendly and graceful kindness to young undergraduates nearly 60 years ago is vivid in the memory of one of them
and I see him, as clearly as I see this sheet of paper, in his surplice
warbling at St. Philip and St. James—which we called by a shorter
name.' Sir Basil has an illuminating story of an encounter with
Hilaire Belloc about 1906. 'Belloc offered my father a collection of
essays. My father undertook to publish them. He then found they
were appearing serially in some literary paper, and he told Belloc
he was disturbed by this. Belloc replied "Oh, that is common form
these days". My father replied "Perhaps I am a little old-fashioned"
and returned the manuscript to him.' Belloc acknowledged defeat,
and by way of amends drew a rebus on his friend's name and composed a Latin hexameter to accompany it: *Sumite Castalios nigris de
fontibus haustus*.[1] The friendship was not disturbed but strengthened,
and Belloc's offering has been reproduced on the cover of many
Blackwell catalogues.

As for the public duties, the Founder undertook these as faithfully
in the life of the city of Oxford as in the world of the book trade.
Apart from his work on the City Council, he was a much-sought-
after treasurer, serving, among others, the Oxford Drama Society,
the Summertown Allotment Association, the University Extension
Movement, and the Oxford Branch of the English Association. He
was a churchwarden for many years, first at St. Mary Magdalen
and later at St. Andrew's, Summertown.

But all these activities were secondary to the main creative purpose
of his life, the bookshop. From the first he stamped his personality
upon it. Books were his delight as well as his business. He wanted
people to buy them, of course, but he liked them to share his pleasure
in handling them, and, indeed, sampling them—though one might
go too far. It was all very well to be able to say 'Oh, I read it in
Blackwell's', but when, on one occasion, the uncut pages of a new
book were found to have been roughly torn, the book was pro-
minently displayed next day with a notice requesting that in future
a paper-knife should be used. It was typical of his way of dealing
with reprehensible behaviour by visitors to his shop—though, to be

[1] 'From the *Black Wells* draw ye the Muses' draughts.'

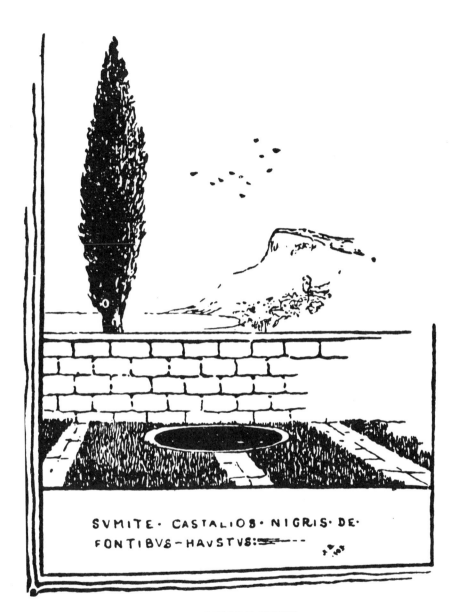

SVMITE · CASTALIOS · NIGRIS · DE · FONTIBVS · HAVSTVS: ═ ── ─

THE BELLOC REBUS

sure, such behaviour was rarer in those days. He kept his temper, and paid the culprit the compliment of assuming him to be not impervious to irony. The method seldom failed. When, one day, the first volume of a set of Swinburne's *Poems* disappeared, an advertisement in the *Oxford Magazine* invited the customer who took the volume to let Mr Blackwell know to what address the remainder of the set might be sent, as the volumes were not sold separately. The missing volume duly reappeared, albeit with a mutilated flyleaf.

His staff learned from him the true Blackwellian attitude to the customer. They learned, also, every detail of their daily work, and they honoured him as a complete bookman and a just and generous employer. He had trained them, like children, in the way that they should go, and he remembered them in his will. Every employee of three years' standing or more received one month's pay as the Founder's farewell gift.

In 1906 this paragraph had appeared in the *Morning Post*: 'Many men will aver that the greatest educative influence of Oxford resides neither in the Bodleian, nor schools, nor tutors, nor lectures, nor college societies, but in the excellent management and liberal facilities of one of the best bookshops in the world—Mr. Blackwell's.'

VII

Basil Blackwell, Publisher
1913–1924

IT was the Founder's plan, as we have seen, that his son should develop the publishing side of the business, and for his first eleven years in Broad Street, until his father's death, he had, in his own words, 'spoken, understood, and thought as a publisher'. He showed at once that he inherited his father's interest in the work of aspiring poets. In his first year he launched the annual series of *Oxford Poetry* that was to be kept up for thirty years more, and was to include among its undergraduate contributors Robert Graves, W. H. Auden, Cecil Day Lewis, Louis MacNeice, and Stephen Spender.

Two more series were started in 1916. One was *Adventurers All*, 'A Series of Young Poets Unknown to Fame'. They included Aldous Huxley, Dorothy L. Sayers, Sacheverell Sitwell, Humbert Wolfe, and E. Powys Mathers (who later won anonymous fame as 'Torquemada' of the *Observer* crosswords). That series of 'slim volumes' ran on bravely, but not very profitably, for eight years, and many of them are now collectors' pieces. Shorter-lived, but not less illustrious by anticipation, was *Wheels*. Basil was becoming known, not only in Oxford, as an enterprising and discriminating friend of poetry. He published Edith Sitwell's first three volumes of poems: *The Mother* (1915), *Twentieth Century Harlequinade* (1916), and *Clowns' Houses* (1918). The 500 copies of *The Mother and other Poems* sold so slowly that there were still 125 left in 1922. Six were bought, for 6*d.* a copy, by S. T. Fenemore,[1] who had a feeling for

[1] See page 68.

poetry. The rest were pulped—and sixty years later a collector would have to pay as much as £140 for this rare book. In 1916 Miss Sitwell brought in the first 'cycle' of *Wheels* to publish, an anthology of new verse by the three Sitwells, Nancy Cunard, E. W. Tennant (whose *Worple Flit and other Poems* Basil had recently published— the author was killed in action in September 1916), and others. Three more cycles were published by Basil: 'The quintessence of Blackwellism' was the *Globe*'s comment on *Wheels 1917*. The fourth (1919) was dedicated 'To the memory of Wilfred Owen, MC' (killed in November 1918) and contained seven of his poems, the first to appear outside periodicals. Basil's 1923 catalogue listed, apart from these series, some fifty other volumes of verse, among them the *Poetical Works* of the American poetess Amy Lowell (1874–1928), of which he had acquired the UK rights in 1920.

It was not only volumes of verse for which the new generation found a sympathetic publisher in Broad Street. Mr Beverley Nichols records in *Who's Who* that at Oxford he was President of the Union, Editor of the *Isis*, and Founder and Editor of the *Oxford Outlook*. This 'little magazine' was launched by Basil Blackwell in the same year, 1919, as J. C. Squire's *London Mercury*. Both rose, phoenix-like, from the ashes of the war, youthful and full of hope. The *Oxford Outlook* appeared once a term, fifty pages or more at 1s. a number (the *London Mercury* cost 36s. a year), and it ran on for nearly twenty years of peace. The editors were sometimes undergraduates, more often young graduates, and Nichols was followed by, among others, Roy Harrod, L. P. Hartley, Julian Huxley, John Betjeman, Graham Greene, Stephen Spender, Isaiah Berlin, Richard Crossman, and John Sparrow. The contributions included short stories, essays, and reviews as well as poetry, and the volumes 'summon up remembrance of things past' with the force of old photographs. Here, as well as the editors, are Siegfried Sassoon, Louis Golding, Edmund Blunden, Richard Hughes, Vera Brittain, Winifred Holtby, Dorothy L. Sayers, Anthony Asquith, W. H. Auden, Cecil Day Lewis, and many others all letting themselves go. Arthur Calder Marshall reviews Bridges' *Testament of Beauty* in 1930 ('in more ways than one a great work'). John Sparrow replies vigorously to an article by a fellow Wykehamist, William Empson, entitled 'O Miselle Passer!' (it was all about an attack by 'poor little Sparrow' on I. A. Richards's *Practical Criticism*). A. L. Rowse writes with mature confidence about 'Shaw and Democracy'. The advertisements are no less nostalgic. In 1926 Minty's announce their easy chair 'The Ely' ('super-resilient upholstery') for £4. 19s. 6d. Richard Goolden, Thea Holme, Veronica Turleigh, Val Gielgud are performing at the old Playhouse in the Woodstock Road. F. T. Long the cutler 'opposite Balliol College' specializes in razor sharpening.

In a special Decennary Number in June 1929 the magazine indulges in some modest self-congratulation. 'The *Oxford Outlook* has gone on for ten years and it will go on . . . so long as there are men and women in the University possessed both of the inclination to write and the endeavour to write well, and so long as the leisure and opportunity to probe as their fancy direct the wide expanses of thought and expression are not altogether crushed underfoot by the Juggernaut's car of the Examination Schools.' (It was a little unfortunate that in that same number the title of a book by Ronald Knox was hilariously misprinted as *Some Loose Stories*.) Vera Brittain, who had come up to Somerville in 1919, wrote 'I went down with the rest of the War generation, and do not know who the next contributors were. But they must have worthily carried on the traditions of their predecessors, for ten years is a long life for so ambitious a University magazine.' True, and it had almost as long to live again. A reviewer in *Discovery* called it 'the most noteworthy of the Oxford undergraduate publications'.

Basil's first editorial assistant was Dorothy L. Sayers ('L' was for Leigh, her mother's maiden name, and must on no account be omitted) who had come up to Somerville before the war to read Modern Languages, in which she obtained a First in 1915—and to sing enthusiastically in the Oxford Bach Choir, as readers of *Gaudy Night* and *Busman's Honeymoon* will have deduced. In 1916 she came to Broad Street to be trained as a publisher, 'a tall, very slim young woman dressed in a formal blue serge costume with informal yellow stockings'. Basil admired her 'witty, lively, gallant mind', but with reservations. 'Her religious convictions were somewhat too

ADRIAN MOTT

obtrusive, and caused me to be provocatively sceptical. She had a crucifix on her desk. I still see her now hammering in one of the nails which had become loose, while continuing an argument on a subject which was in no sense religious. . . . She kissed me when my son Richard was born. At the end of some three years I had to tell her that it was not fair to expect her to become a steady efficient publisher. It was like harnessing a racehorse to a plough.' In 1920 she joined the advertising firm of S. H. Benson—and gathered copy for *Murder must Advertise*.

Miss Sayers was succeeded by Basil's old friend from Merton days, Adrian Mott, and the publishing business, which had been run as a separate department by Basil since 1913, began to show outward and visible signs of independence. The imprint on the books was changed from 'Blackwell' to 'Basil Blackwell', and two years later the two friends entered into a formal partnership as Basil Blackwell and Mott Ltd., incorporated on 13 March 1922. They were already fellow directors (Basil Blackwell as Chairman) of the Shakespeare Head Press Company formed in 1921, the story of which is told in the next chapter.

Sir Adrian Mott (he succeeded his father as second baronet in 1938) was a lovable and very consistent character. 'I felt I had lost a benevolent uncle' one of his colleagues, James Sherbourn, wrote after his death in 1964. Sir Basil paid a moving tribute to him in the form of a letter to 'My Dear Old Man' from which some extracts may be quoted.

You asked me (in 1919) if I could give you some insight of publishing and I, recalling a diverting breakfast party in Merton a year or so after I had gone down at which I was impressed by your spontaneous parody of Oscar Wilde, thought that you might have a bent for such a career and invited you to come and try your hand.

So I had the happy experience of daily contact with you, and so our friendship grew until you held a unique place in my affection. I had often wished that I had a brother and in our relationship came to regard you in that light. We could talk together without reserve and say things to each other with a frankness peculiar to that standing. Even now I can hear you say, 'When the old man begins to pronounce blameless principles I know he is meditating something sly.' There was an integrity in your judgements which was valuable to me, and you became to no small extent the keeper of my business and aesthetic conscience.

Mott was a deliberate, not to say slow, worker, and his reluctance, almost inability, to finish a piece of work on time, or at all, taxed the patience of his more businesslike colleagues, but 'mutual confidence and good fellowship reigned'.

It was enjoyable, and certainly meritorious, to encourage young talent in Oxford, but it was far from profitable. It was the publishers in London who reaped the fruits of Basil's labour, for they could hold out the lure of a famous imprint, and they had, in those days, better means of distribution. It was mortifying to see the names of the young authors whose first work had come out under the Blackwell imprint soon appearing in the lists of Macmillan, Faber, Cape, and the rest. *Sic vos non vobis mellificatis apes.*[1] It was clear that if Basil was to hold his authors he must move to London himself. There was plenty of evidence of the public's strong interest in poetry. Harold Monro had started the Poetry Bookshop in Devonshire Street near Holborn just before the war, and the anthologies of *Georgian Poetry*, edited by 'E.M.' (Sir Edward Marsh), that he published between 1912 and 1922 sold nearly 20,000 copies each within a few years. J. C. (Sir John) Squire's *Selections from Modern Poets* (Martin Secker, 1921) achieved even wider success. But a London base was needed for these enterprises, and Basil was anchored to Oxford by the bookshop, where he would soon have to succeed his father as head of the business. Moreover, 'Modern Poetry' was beginning to mean something different. Clough, invoking the Poet of the Future some seventy years earlier, had written

> Come, Poet, come! Our real and inner deeds rehearse,
> And make our meaning clear in verse,

but enthusiasm for the Poet of the Present was not nourished by the increasing difficulty of understanding him. Marsh, in his prefatory note to *Georgian Poetry 1920–1922* (the last of the series), replied firmly to critics who were beginning to complain that he was behind the

[1] 'Thus not for you, ye bees, ye honey make.'

times. 'Much admired modern work seem to me, in its lack of inspiration and its disregard of form, like gravy imitating lava.'

Basil turned to other fields of publishing. There had long been a rival to poetry in his affections. In 1907 he had chosen, as part of a school prize, William Morris's *The Earthly Paradise*, and this had led him to the prose romances and so to Mackail's *Life of William Morris*. There he learnt about the Kelmscott Press, and a flame was kindled. Soon after joining his father in Broad Street he had come across, among the second-hand books, a special number of the *Studio* of 1911 devoted to book production. An article on fine printing by Bernard Newdigate caught his eye, an encounter which was to lead, after the war, to his acquisition and revival of the Shakespeare Head Press.

Meanwhile he decided to make some experiments, in which he was encouraged and generously advised by Emery Walker.[1] In 1914 he brought out a new edition of a Portuguese story, *The Sweet Miracle*, translated by Edgar Prestage, in a pretty Royal 16mo, priced at 1s. 'Type and printing almost worthy of the Kelmscott Press, but easier to read' wrote the *Bristol Times* reviewer, and a reprint was called for two years later. The autumn list of 1917, in a conspicuously new format and set in Dolphin Old Style type, announced the forthcoming *Sheldonian Series* of reprints of 'short masterpieces in all languages' to be printed in that same type on handmade paper, in editions of 500 copies: little books (one of them was the *Funeral Oration of Pericles* from Hobbes's translation of Thucydides) which sold out rapidly.

But weightier matters were in preparation. Basil had inherited a bookman's enthusiasm that looked before as well as after. There were old authors, as well as young, to be encouraged, good books long out of print to be revived, writers whose collected works deserved new editions. The Founder had reprinted in 1898 George Herbert's serene prose 'character' of the country parson, *A Priest to the Temple* (1652), edited by H. C. Beeching. Basil now planned a

1 Sir Emery Walker (1851–1933), the most influential typographer of his day; originator, with William Morris, of the Kelmscott Press and co-founder, with Cobden Sanderson, of the Doves Press.

whole series of such scholarly reprints, under the general editorship of another and more recent friend of the firm, H. F. B. Brett-Smith, of Corpus Christi College and later Goldsmith Reader in English Literature. These were the *Percy Reprints* of English classics 'for the most part unobtainable'. The first three appeared in 1920, and seven more by the end of the period covered by this chapter. The series won the high reputation it deserved as a fine enterprise of non-commercial scholarly publishing. The most notable item was a two-volume edition of Etherege's plays and poems, the first definitive collected edition, published in 1927.

Apart from these three fields—of new poetry (which proved unfruitful), in fine printing, and English classics (which were to be combined in the Shakespeare Head publications)—there was an important group of Virgilian studies. Among the dons who had sometimes brought their books to be published from Broad Street were some very well-known Oxford characters. The eminent historian C. H. Firth was a familiar figure in the shop, with an endearing habit of coming back to look for his umbrella, only to find that it was on his arm all the time, underneath his gown. Another was W. Warde Fowler of Lincoln College. His first book, *A Year with the Birds*, had sold so well that it had been transferred to Macmillan's, but a second was less successful. 'The sale of the *Marsh Warbler* has been astonishingly small' he wrote to Blackwell in 1894. In his old age, and in retirement, he brought three studies of the *Aeneid* to be published from Broad Street between 1915 and 1919. There he found a publisher whose interest in Virgil was lifelong, and who was elected President of the Classical Association fifty years later. Warde Fowler's books inaugurated a notable series of *Virgilian Studies* which in a few years contained more than a dozen volumes by various hands.

In 1914 Basil had married Marion Christine Soans and they founded a thriving family. A Blackwellian remembered seeing 'B.B.'s children romping along, sometimes barefooted, on the pavement' and B.B. himself greeting their approach: 'Oh dear, here come the Philistines.' He had, therefore, a sound domestic motive when he moved into the field of what the trade used to call 'juveniles'—and gave the name *Joy Street* to an annual that made its first appearance in 1923. *Number 1 Joy Street* set a new standard for children's books. The Annuals of those days—Herbert Strang's from the Oxford University Press was one of the best—were beloved by children and contained some good stuff, but the general literary level was mediocre or worse and the illustrations and format no better. Basil decided that children deserved, and might enjoy, something of a higher order. The authors whom he enlisted to write for *Joy Street* included Hilaire Belloc, G. K. Chesterton, Walter de la Mare, Eleanor Farjeon, Rose Fyleman, Laurence Housman, Compton Mackenzie, and A. A. Milne, whose first children's classic, *When We Were Very Young*, came out in the same year as *No. 2 Joy Street*. The annual appeared punctually year by year until 1935.

Joy Street was a resounding success, and Basil produced many other children's books notable for their high quality in matter and format. The same quest for excellence led him into the field of books for the school as well as the nursery. The time was propitious. H. A. L. Fisher's Education Act of 1918 had made school attendance until 14 compulsory and thereby increased the elementary school population, at the upper end, by about a quarter of a million. The first steps were also being taken towards the ideal of 'Secondary Education for All' set out in R. H. Tawney's policy statement for the Labour Party. Elementary schools were being divided into Junior (up to 11) and Senior (11 plus). New, and better, and more, books were needed for the reorganized and larger schools.

It was then that Basil decided to have a look at the school text-book field. 'I visited a local educational supplier and spent £1 on an armful of them for examination. It was a shocking experience. The dominant consideration was cheapness, and to this were sacrificed the contents physical and intellectual. The ruling impression was of hack work shoddily produced.' Strong words, and it may be urged for the defence that teachers and publishers alike were still feeling their way. But Basil had a point, and he was soon able to prove it.

About 1920 he met a progressive and shrewd Inspector of elementary schools, E. H. Carter, who encouraged him to enter this field of publishing and undertook to advise him. Carter introduced

Ernest Wilfred Parker, educational manager of Collins, whose contract was due for renewal. In the event he decided not to renew it but to join Blackwell, and when, in 1922, the firm of Basil Blackwell and Mott Ltd. was formed, Parker became a director. 'It was one of the wisest and happiest decisions in my business life,' writes Sir Basil. 'Voluble, cheerfully aggressive, endowed with a brilliant mind and seemingly complete self-assurance, he was a master of the technique of elementary school book publishing, which he had adopted as a career after some years in the teaching profession. . . . He had hosts of friends in his educational field and his energy seemed illimitable. He was not the easiest of colleagues, but our debt to him was immense.'

Parker's health broke down after his wife's death in 1929 and he died four years later after a long nervous illness, but he had lived to see his firm make a spectacular entry into the educational field. In 1925 the first volume appeared of the Marten and Carter *Histories* for Senior (elementary) Schools, and Basil had proved his point. The 'infant firm', which had been making slow progress after the difficult war years, now began to prosper—but the era ushered in by Marten and Carter belongs to a later chapter.

Basil Blackwell and Mott (generally B & M hereafter) occupied 49 Broad Street, paying a rent of £50 a year to the parent business. No. 49 had a frontage of about ten feet, with William Hunt's typewriter shop and typing school next door in No. 48, and was separated from Blackwell's at ground level by the narrow passage leading to Bliss Court. There was a connecting corridor on the first floor between the bookshop and the publishing offices.

The staff in 1922 consisted of S. T. Fenemore, three girls, Frank Fogden (who left three years later), and a boy. The boy spent too much of his employers' time practising the ukulele in the basement and was replaced in 1923 by R. H. (James) Sherbourn. Fenemore, known throughout the publishing side of the firm as 'Fen', had joined Blackwell's in 1912. He was a man of total integrity, brisk and dapper with a precise turn of mind and a short turn of phrase. He organized an extremely efficient warehouse and inspired affection as well as awe. His discipline was strict—people were instructed to 'keep moving, don't let your braces dangle!' Occasionally he would produce some odd piece of advice, telling, for instance, a colleague about to check stock in the basement not to be alarmed if he saw a very old rat emerge from between the packets of Chancellor's Latin Verse and Gaisford Greek Prose prize competition: 'He is quite harmless. You will recognize him by his yellow tusks, and the small wooden crutch under his left foreleg which aids his progress along the hot pipes, the warmth of which comforts his rheumatics.' At heart Fen was a poet. It was he who bought those last six copies of Edith Sitwell's *The Mother* and gave copies to his family and colleagues.

One could not find a more devoted member of the firm, and it was characteristic of his courage and attitude to life that at the farewell dinner given to mark his retirement after fifty years' service to the firm, on the morning of which he had been told he had terminal cancer, he still managed a stream of witty barracking during every speech in his honour.

Sherbourn, who ended up as a Director, and Secretary to the Company, had started as the odd-job boy, one of whose duties was to fetch Chelsea buns from Week's shop in Cornmarket for the Directors' tea. He was one of a family of nine, the son of a GWR railwayman who lived in Witney. His name was Reginald, and there are two stories of how he came by the name that was to stick to him for all his time in the firm. The first is that Basil Blackwell on hearing his name paused and said 'I shall call you James'. The other is that running down the passageway between Bliss Court and the main building, he nearly knocked down Basil's formidable secretary, Miss Lovelace, who asked, not knowing his name, 'Where are you going to, young James?' Be that as it may, James he became and remained, gradually taking over the book-keeping and accounts. He became a Sgt. Air Mechanic in the RAF in the war and rejoined the firm in peacetime to look after wages and accounts.

He was one of the kindliest, sweetest-natured, and most cheerful of men, ready to turn a hand to any job. His neat handwriting was an example to everyone and his maps, diagrams, and marginal drawings were used extensively in the production of Carter and Brentnall's

Geography series *Man the World Over*. He and his wife were enthusiasts for Old Time Dancing, and he prided himself on his physical fitness, beating his chest and saying 'Six foot of whipcord and spring steel'. He never flapped, never raised his voice, never lost his temper, and is remembered affectionately by all who knew him.

VIII

The Shakespeare Head Press

TOWARDS the end of the summer of 1903, A. H. Bullen, publisher, of 47 Great Russell Street, London, dreamt that he was on a visit to Stratford-upon-Avon, and that just as he was leaving, someone approached him, saying "You must have a copy of this before you go: look, SHAKESPEARE's Works, printed here, by his fellow-townsmen!" A.H.B. remembers thinking in his dream, "By Jove, that is a good idea: I must remember that when I wake". The following morning, he revealed the scheme to me, as his partner.' Thus wrote that partner, Frank Sidgwick, in the diary that records how, between May 1904 and March 1905, the dream began to come true.[1] Within a few months, they had found premises in Stratford, 21 Chapel Street, where Julius Shaw, the first witness to Shakespeare's will, had lived, and only two doors away from Shakespeare's own house, New Place.

By 1907 the publication of the *Stratford Town Shakespeare* was completed. Starting from scratch, or behind it, he had prepared and annotated the text, and five Stratford craftsmen had printed it in the parlour, kitchen, bedrooms, and attics of an Elizabethan dwelling-house in the space of three years—nearly 4,000 pages in ten volumes.

Bullen deserves to be better known today. His editions of the sixteenth- and seventeenth-century plays and poems have been superseded by the work of later scholars, but he was a notable pioneer. His publication of *Lyrics from the Song-books of the Elizabethan Age* in 1886 enabled Palgrave to include in the second edition

---

[1] *Frank Sidgwick's Diary and other material relating to A. H. Bullen and the Shakespeare Head Press*: Basil Blackwell, 1975. Sidgwick left Bullen in 1908 and founded the firm of Sidgwick and Jackson.

21 CHAPEL STREET, STRATFORD–UPON–AVON

of the *Golden Treasury* (1891) such now well-known pieces as 'Fain would I change that note' and 'Weep you no more, sad fountains'. Ten years later Quiller-Couch acknowledged the same debt in his preface to the *Oxford Book of English Verse*. Bullen pointed the way for musicians too. A study of the lyrics which he had rescued from three centuries of oblivion led Frederick Keel to look into the song-books themselves 'with a hope that the music might be found to be as fine as the words'. It was, and in 1909 he brought out his first set of *Elizabethan Love Songs*, which, in turn, led to E. H. Fellowes's monumental edition of these long-forgotten works in 68 volumes.

Bullen, alas, had no head for commerce. Yeats wrote to a friend that he had 'the greatest possible contempt for my dear Bullen's business capacity'. His Press was soon in difficulties. Capital was essential to produce books so lavishly and sell them so slowly (nearly half the edition of 1,000 copies of the *Shakespeare* were still unsold in 1915), and Bullen had none. Attempts to raise an endowment by public subscription, notably in 1916, the tercentenary year of Shakespeare's death, were a dismal failure. When Bullen died in 1919, aged 63, the Press was virtually bankrupt.

It is at this point that Basil Blackwell comes into the story. It looked as if it was all up with the Shakespeare Head Press. An Indian Maharajah had some thought of acquiring the premises as a training school for Indian printers, and Thomas Jones[1] wanted to buy the equipment to start the Gregynog Press in Wales. But rescuers were found. Emery Walker was consulted, and it was probably he who suggested that his young friend Blackwell might be interested. Bullen's executors approached him, he and Mott went to Stratford to see how things stood, and, in his own words 'we decided to form a little company to develop the ideas which had inspired the founder. H. F. B. Brett-Smith, who wrote the article on Bullen in the *DNB*, was to guide us in matters of scholarship. H. S. Critchley was to watch over our accounts; Benjamin Chandler, dilettante and patron of fine printing, furnished a helpful measure of finance; I hoped that

---

[1] Thomas Jones ('T.J.'), CH (1870–1955), sometime Deputy Secretary of the Cabinet, lifelong promoter of adult education and founder of Coleg Harlech, and a moving spirit on innumerable charitable bodies.

my experience in publishing would help in the business of publicity and distribution, but the keystone was the typographical genius of the scholar-printer Bernard Newdigate.'

The business was purchased for £1,500 and the Shakespeare Head Press Limited (hereinafter SHP) was incorporated on 21 February 1921. The authorized share capital was £2,500, of which £1,950 had so far been subscribed, £1,000 of it by Chandler, and when the second directors' meeting was held in June only £20 was left in the bank. Appeals to the Stratford brewer Mr Flower and to the elderly novelist Marie Corelli[1] were equally unsuccessful, and shortage of working capital was to worry the directors for several years. But the achievements of the SHP are more important for posterity than the financial and commercial skills that supported them.

The rescue of the Press was, at the time, an act of faith, taken, moreover, at the start of a year that the *Economist* called 'one of the worst years of depression since the Industrial Revolution' (there were over two million unemployed in June 1921). But the time was more propitious than the rescuers, perhaps, realized. Hitherto the interest in fine printing that had been stirred up by William Morris (his book, the Kelmscott *Chaucer*, came out in the year he died, 1896) was confined to a small number of connoisseurs. The books of the Doves Press (Emery Walker and Cobden-Sanderson) and the Ashendene Press (St. John Hornby), both established soon after Morris's death, were, like the Kelmscott books, expensive limited editions, by their very nature not available, and little known, to the general public. Most printers went on printing books as their fathers had before them and the public, knowing no better, were content. But not for long. Blackwell himself, as we have seen, was one of those who had begun, some years earlier, to tempt them with less conservative typography. Francis Meynell broke new ground by his foundation of the Nonesuch Press in 1923. It was not a press in the Kelmscott (or Doves or Ashendene) sense, but a publishing house;

[1] Marie Corelli (Miss Mary Mackay) had made a fortune out of such best-sellers as *The Sorrows of Satan* (1895), one of the first novels to appear in a single volume (instead of three), at 6s. She had settled in Stratford in 1901, and became a generous but wayward benefactor of her adopted town. She died in 1924.

Meynell had no printing press of his own, and his books were printed by many different firms, including the University Presses of Oxford and Cambridge, but all of them, various as they were, bore the mark of his expert taste. The public responded enthusiastically.

It was becoming good business, not simple idealism, to be generous of time and skill in the design of books. Two new publishers of the 1920s, Jonathan Cape and Geoffrey Faber, applied the principle to the whole of their output. The two ancient University Presses 'renewed their youth', as Newdigate wrote in a survey of fine printing in Great Britain from 1925 to 1934, and took 'an active and leading part in the new movement'. Modern machinery, moreover, was for once on the side of the angels. The Lanston Monotype Company, under the expert and persuasive guidance of Stanley Morison, revived many historical types and introduced many new ones specially designed for them. The resources of printers were enlarged and improved out of all recognition.

Thus it was that the SHP entered on a new lease of life in a world that was developing a welcome appetite for fine printing. The genius of Bernard Newdigate, 'keystone' of the enterprise, was to have full play for more than twenty happy and active years. His life and work have been commemorated by his old friend Joseph Thorp (*B. H. Newdigate, Scholar-Printer 1869–1944*: Blackwell, 1950) and by Basil Blackwell in an article in *Signature* (July 1946).

Bernard Henry Newdigate was of the same kin as the Sir Roger Newdigate who founded the well-known prize for English Verse at Oxford in 1806. Blackwell has written, elsewhere, of the man himself.

His thoughts, words, and deeds always appeared to me to be controlled by a spirit trained in obedience to the highest loyalties. There was no extravagance in him. His speech was short, simple, and pointed. I never heard a violent or ribald phrase. He would have gone to the stake for his religious faith, but he held it without bigotry. He admitted the expression of any honest opinion, and was intolerant only of what was manifestly corrupt. Then his refusal was absolute. In his bearing there was no variation; it was that of a man at peace with himself, and so disciplined that he could give his whole mind to his company or to the matter in hand.

He received a sound classical education at Stonyhurst and read Greek and Latin with enjoyment till the end of his life. He was widely read in English literature, his chief interest lying, like Bullen's, in the sixteenth and seventeenth centuries. He played a large part in the completion of the SHP edition of *Drayton* (left unfinished by the death of its editor, Professor J. W. Hebel), and himself wrote a supplementary volume on *Michael Drayton and his Circle*. He was, in short, a scholar-printer in the tradition of Caxton—and Bullen. But, if Bullen was the better scholar, he can hardly be compared with Newdigate as a printer.

Newdigate was a professional where Bullen was an amateur. He had been a printer for twenty-five years 'and lost money at it', as he told Blackwell at their first meeting. He learned the craft in his father's small printing and publishing business at Leamington, out of which grew the *Arden Press*, taken over by W. H. Smith in 1905. There, with guidance and encouragement from that father-figure of the typographical revival, Emery Walker, he produced much distinguished work, but his printing career was interrupted by the 1914–18 war, throughout which, though well over age, he served as an infantry officer. In 1920, at Sir John Squire's invitation, he began a series of Book Production Notes in the *London Mercury*, which won him such an outstanding reputation as a typographical critic that for the next eighteen years every important finely printed book came to the *Mercury* office to be reviewed by him. In the same year came the invitation from Blackwell to be master printer at the SHP.

'His scholarship was so unobtrusive that one lost sight of it, perhaps, in admiration of his technical accomplishments. He set definite limits to his range in typography, but within that range he produced magnificently printed books that had astonishing variety and perfect fitness to their texts, and they will always rank among the finest products of the modern revival' wrote the eminent American typographer Bruce Rogers. No doubt he had chiefly in mind the noble quartos, which included the *Froissart* (8 vols., 1927–8), *Chaucer* (8 vols., 1928–9), *Spenser* (8 vols., 1930), Chapman's *Homer* (5 vols., 1930–1), and *Drayton* (5 vols., 1941). Newdigate himself, writing in

1935, was inclined to think that the *Froissart* (with an exemplary index made by Basil's wife, Christine) was still the best of them. This sumptuous edition of Berners's translation of the *Chronycle*, first printed by Pynson in 1520–3, was embellished with many hundreds of coats of arms, all coloured by hand 'in their proper tinctures'. Lord Berners had made his translation at the instance of Henry VIII, and the SHP reprint was dedicated, by permission, to George V. His Majesty was more gracious than his father had been. When Frank Sidgwick wrote to seek permission to dedicate the *Stratford Town Shakespeare* to Edward VII the reply came back that His Majesty only accepted the dedication of works by authors with whom he was personally acquainted.

'At first all the setting was done by hand,' writes Sir Basil, 'but it was soon manifest that if Newdigate had to design and print a single volume for sale at a moderate price, such was his care to "get it right" that either the Press or the publisher, or both, must make a loss. The solution lay in the planning of a series of uniform volumes and was achieved in the SHP editions of the eighteenth-century novelists.' Smollet (11 vols.) in 1925–6 was followed by Fielding (10 vols., 1926), Sterne (7 vols., 1926–7), Defoe (14 vols., 1927–8), Richardson (18 vols., 1929–30), and Swift (14 vols., 1939–68). Trollope's *Barchester* novels (14 vols., 1929) and the Brontës (19 vols., 1932–6) were in the same series. 'The setting of these many volumes was beyond the scope of the hand compositors, and most of the work was done by Monotype at Bristol and Oxford.'

Apart from these two groups of books, its most characteristic productions, Newdigate designed many others for the SHP, from *Pindar's Odes of Victory* in the New Hellenic type of the Monotype Corporation, with C. J. Billson's translation *en face*, or *The School for Scandal* with decorations by Thomas Lowinsky, to small books of new poetry, one of which was Mr Enoch Powell's *First Poems*.

It remains to tell the story of the book that Blackwell himself considers Newdigate's 'worthiest achievement in type'. It is certainly the best known, for many more copies of it have been sold than of all the other SHP books put together.

Newdigate's skill in designing for Malory's *Morte d'Arthur* (1935) a quarto page which, though set in double column, was good to look at as well as easy to read, fired Blackwell with the idea of attempting a one-volume Shakespeare. After weeks of trial Newdigate produced a Royal 8vo page in 9-pt. Plantin that seemed the very thing. The whole of Shakespeare could be got into 1260 pages. The questions were, how many to print, and what price to sell at? It so happened that the newspaper proprietors were in the middle of a circulation war, and were offering sets of Dickens, encyclopaedias, and other literary furniture to the public in exchange for a few coupons and a small cash payment. The *Daily Mail* had just fired off an offer of a complete Shakespeare for 5s. 9d. and six coupons. Blackwell decided to defy them. He found that if he printed 50,000 copies he could sell at 6s. and he put it to Mott. 'Tell me, old man,' said Mott, 'if we should not sell a single copy, should we go bust?' 'No.' 'Then let's do it.' And they did. The work was farmed out to Billing of Guildford and pushed through at a pace which forbade 'fidgeting' with the proofs, and published in 1935. The public bought all 50,000 and a reprint was brought out two years later. The book was far superior to, and as cheap as, the much-trumpeted offers of the newspapers, and the circulation battle of the books was called off.

To complete the story, in 1940 the type moulds were destroyed in an air raid, but Newdigate lived to see the book reappear, reset, with an introductory life of Shakespeare written by himself, in the last year of his life, 1944. It was his last production for the SHP as the *Stratford Town Shakespeare* had been Bullen's first.

The management of the business side of the SHP had not been plain sailing. When the new Company was formed in 1921 the Directors had a number of problems to face. Bullen's plant at Stratford could produce well enough the fine books that would justify Newdigate's appointment, and carry on and develop the founder's aims, but it could not compete effectively with more up-to-date printers in producing the kind of work that would bring grist to the mill. Successful expansion or even adaption were impracticable in the cramped premises of 21 Chapel Street. There had never been an efficient organization for distribution and publicity, and there was no room for that, either. Most serious of all was the lack of capital.

The question of distribution and publicity was soon settled. B & M became publishers to the Press and SHP books appeared regularly in their lists from 1922 onwards. They shouldered some of the financial burden, too; in 1923 the Directors formally resolved that B & M be authorized to publish books with the SHP imprint at their own expense, subject to the Board's approval, and as time went on more and more of the financial responsibility was thus transferred to B & M.

The drawbacks of the plant and premises at Stratford remained. The Secretary, W. W. Blair-Fish, lost little time in proposing that the Press should be moved to Oxford. The fine books could be printed there more conveniently in modern premises, and other books, bringing quicker returns, could be farmed out, under Newdigate's supervision, to printers better equipped for such work. But the Directors were not yet ready to abandon the birthplace of the Press—and of Shakespeare—with the traditions and associations that had been so valuable to it. Newdigate need not move to Oxford in order to design and supervise the production of 'bread and butter' books, and, as we have seen, several series of such books were soon being planned and launched from the Stratford headquarters.

The SHP, however, still failed to pay its way, and in 1928 the Directors determined to see whether the move to Oxford, proposed six years earlier, would improve matters. Apart from the gain in efficiency to be expected from more convenient quarters and from bringing printing and publishing together in one place, where most of the Directors lived, Newdigate himself wanted to move away from Stratford for the sake of his wife's health. The search for suitable premises began, and in May 1930 the SHP moved to 33 St. Aldate's, above the Kemp Hall Press, where the Company became the tenants of the proprietors, Messrs Fox Jones Ltd. Some forty tons of material—machinery, type, and paper—were conveyed from Stratford and duly installed in one week at the cost of £50 to the removal firm and about £300 for installation. Printing began again on 27 May, and the future looked brighter.

But not for long. The following year the great economic depression that had burst over America in 1929 spread across the Atlantic, and the demand for fine books and other luxuries was sharply reduced. In 1932, the SHP's machines were idle for much of the year and the Company lost more than £1,000. B & M again came to the rescue. The firm had been expanding rapidly since the launching of the Marten and Carter Histories for schools in 1925, and some of its increasing output of new books was sent to be printed in St. Aldate's to keep the machines running. This was all very well as means to an end, but the central purpose of the SHP was, as ever, to produce limited editions of fine books. If it were enabled to carry on doing so, on however modest a scale, in the hope of better days to come, the means would be justified. But better days did not come. By 1938 it was clear, as the Minute Book states, that 'the market for fine books of a literary character had practically ceased to exist'.

The war was the final blow. In 1942 the St. Aldate's premises were requisitioned for war purposes, the plant sold, and the Press became, in effect, a subsidiary publishing department of B & M. The Company remained in being, with its separate Board and accounts, and the name was kept alive (SHP Books for Children, including some by Enid Blyton, were a successful venture), but the Shakespeare Head Press of Bullen and Newdigate was no more.

IX

Mr Basil takes Charge
1924–1939

THE fifteen years between the Founder's death and the outbreak of war in 1939 were far from tranquil. The Great Depression of 1931 sent the number of unemployed up to nearly three million, drove Britain off the gold standard, and reduced the value of the pound abroad by a third. In 1936, the nation was deeply shaken by the abdication crisis, and the closing years were darkened by the threat of war. The effects of these great disturbances in the realm can be plainly seen in the annual accounts of B. H. Blackwell. Things went well until 1931, turnover increasing steadily by about £6,000 a year, from £60,000 to £95,000. Then came the slump, and it took five years to climb slowly to £100,000. Thereafter business revived, only to fall off again in the last two years. Turnover in the year before the war had reached £118,000.

In those days of stable prices, money growth and real growth meant the same thing. Blackwell's were selling twice as many books in 1939 as in 1924. That was an achievement that few booksellers could match. The years between the slump and the war were 'a period of stress and decline for British booksellers. I would hazard the statement that very many, if not the majority, of booksellers at that time would have welcomed some form of takeover.'[1] Still, it came as a shock to the Trade when the famous old firm of Hatchard's in Piccadilly succumbed. A financier, Clarence Hatry, who had been serving a prison sentence for fraud, was released in 1938 when fresh evidence came to light, and turned his attention to the ailing book

---

[1] Basil Blackwell.

trade. His first enterprise was to buy Hatchard's, in partnership with Sir Thomas Moore, a Member of Parliament who had campaigned vigorously for his release. Hatry actually made a personal approach to Blackwell, which was firmly rejected, but he was not discouraged, and sent a circular letter to many other members of the Booksellers' Association, offering to take them over. But he was just too late. The war, as we shall see, came to the rescue, and his only other notable acquisition was the purchase of the well-known City firm of Stoneham's in the aftermath of the disastrous German incendiary raid of 29 December 1940.

Great efforts were needed in Broad Street, before the war, to keep sales level, or better than level. 'I remember addressing my colleagues at the beginning of the 1931 slump, telling them that we must now force sales by careful attention to individuals' interests, to be recorded by the addressograph',[1] a novel piece of equipment bought for £500. So the advertising department was reorganized, and while booksellers everywhere watched their sales falling, Blackwell's actually increased a little. But though turnover doubled between 1924 and 1939, profits were falling. In the first half of the period they averaged £8,000 a year, in the second only £7,500, on a larger turnover, in fact a decline from over 10 per cent of turnover to under 7 per cent. By the time directors' fees and dividends had been paid there was little left for capital growth and expansion. Booksellers in general were suffering from a kind of indigestion brought on by a surfeit of new books. It was, of course, nothing new for them to be handling a commodity with a very large variety of items, and, except for schoolbooks, sold one at a time. Even in Victorian days the number of new books published each year had risen to 5,000. In 1939 it was 18,000.

Fiction accounted for more than a quarter of this total, though most of the five thousand titles published each year were produced for the lending libraries, not for the bookshops. An annual contributor was P. G. Wodehouse, then, to use one of his favourite expressions, in mid-season form. Belloc had called him the best writer of English alive, and in 1939 he appeared, shyly, at the

[1] Basil Blackwell.

Encaenia in Oxford to be made Doctor of Letters *honoris causa*. Some of the new writers most praised by the critics (but not most bought by the public) were becoming less romantic and more outspoken. It was no longer true, as Walter Bagehot had written some seventy years earlier, that only 'French writers, whom we will not name, enhanced the interest of their narratives by trading on the excitement of stimulating scenes', though D. H. Lawrence could only get *Lady Chatterly's Lover* published in France. But the general reader's favourite kind of fiction became the detective story. Sherlock Holmes had stood almost alone, but he was now followed by scores of ingenious sleuths, headed by Hercule Poirot and Lord Peter Wimsey.

Far behind adult fiction, but in second place, came children's books, of which about fifteen hundred were now appearing each year. A. A. Milne's and Arthur Ransome's became classics in their kind, and in 1937 *The Hobbit* first made the name of Tolkien famous.

The new poets seemed to come mostly from Oxford. Auden, Day-Lewis, McNeice, and Spender all went up to the university in the twenties. So did John Betjeman. Eliot and Blunden had been up just before the war and Graves came up, from the trenches, just after. It was a remarkable array of diverse talents—and most of them, as we have seen, had had their earliest poems published by Basil Blackwell while still undergraduates. But it was a very much older Oxford poet, Robert Bridges, who, at the age of eighty-five, produced the surprise of the inter-war period. *The Testament of Beauty* (1929) sold more copies on publication than any other long poem since *Don Juan*.

Biography, history, religion, science, technology, in all these fields books came pouring from the publishers. More titles to stock meant more shelf space and more—and better qualified, and better paid—staff to handle them. No wonder the trade complained of indigestion and rising overheads. Blackwell's rose from 15 per cent to 20 per cent in Basil's first fifteen years as Chairman, and he seldom let an Annual General Meeting pass without drawing attention to it.

Another hardy annual in the Minute Book is the burden of outstanding credit accounts. In 1925, book debts amounted to £30,000.

'Something should be done', the Directors agreed, 'to dispel the popular delusion that unlimited credit could be obtained from the Company.' Something was done. The Chairman urged Charles Field, ever optimistic about his debtors, to sterner measures, and himself wrote letters to the worst offenders. Undergraduates were warned that they must settle their bills at the end of each term. Things did not continue to get worse, but they did not get much better. It came to be accepted that the proportion of book debts to turnover was not likely to be brought much below 40 per cent. It was 37 per cent in 1939.

The educational publishers benefited greatly from the post-war reforms in education. There were less than 200,000 children in the grant-aided secondary schools in 1914. In 1935, there were nearly half a million, in many more schools. The increasing population of better-educated young citizens emerging from these schools were a welcome addition to the book-buying public, but first more school-books were needed. More were needed, too, for the other children over eleven now catered for in the reorganized Senior Schools. There it was a question not just of more books for more children but of new kinds of books. The Senior School pupil was a new species, who needed something different from the Grammar School pupil of the same age. It was to supply this new need that Blackwell, as publisher, first entered the educational field.

The opening of the story has been briefly told in Chapter VII. Blackwell decided to begin with a history series, and he went to see C. H. K. (later Sir Henry) Marten at Eton. Marten was a first-rate historian and a remarkable and influential teacher, and had, with Townsend Warner, written one of the most widely used textbooks for grammar and public schools, *The Groundwork of British History* (1912). He became President of the Historical Association from 1929 to 1931, was entrusted by King George V with the historical education of the twelve-year-old Princess Elizabeth in 1938, and became provost of Eton in 1945. He was fired with enthusiasm for Blackwell's idea, but he had no first-hand knowledge of the needs of the Senior schools. E. H. Carter, H.M.I., who had read history as a scholar of Jesus College at Cambridge, could supply the missing expertise and was brought in as joint author. 'Marten and Carter' was to become as well known as 'Warner and Marten'. The first book appeared in 1925 and the series of four was completed in 1927. It was an immediate success, 'so unusually good as to out-distance all else of the kind', as the educational reviewer in the *Spectator* proclaimed. Each volume was soon selling at the rate of a thousand a week. A good foundation on which to build an educational list.

Marten and Carter for the seniors was followed by a history series for juniors by Laurence Housman and Marten. There were readers, story books, and collections of poetry galore. A very big seller was *A Short Bible*, based on the recommendations of a consultative committee set up by the churches, the selections chosen and arranged by a distinguished team of editors, of whom one was the headmaster of the Dragon School at Oxford, A. E. Lynam. *Man the World Over* by Carter and Brentnall did well in the field of geography and marked a notable advance in presentation and the use of photographs. The books from Broad Street had a freshness of approach that won them wide recognition, not only in the text but in the illustrations by such artists as Hugh Chesterman, L. R. Brightwell, and C. T. Nightingale. But Blackwell's most ambitious project, after Marten and Carter, was somewhat of a disappointment. The *Introduction to Science* gave shape to the new conception of 'General Science' for the senior schools and the authors were two eminent scientists, E. N. Da C. Andrade and Julian Huxley. But the series came out too slowly—four volumes spread over the five years 1931 to 1935— and its failure to live up to the high hopes of publisher and authors was at any rate partly due to the slump of 1931. Local Education Authorities cut their book grants by 10 per cent, sometimes much more, and sales of schoolbooks, especially new ones, were severely affected. At the end of 1936, the Chairman told his fellow directors that even Marten and Carter seemed to have 'reached saturation point', but, happily, it was still going strong thirty years later, by which time the total sales were approaching two million.

If a publisher is to prosper he needs a thriving back-list of perennials, or an annual crop of quick profit-makers, or both. Until he broke into the schoolbook field Blackwell had not enough of either. His children's books—the 'juveniles'—more than paid their way, but there were other kinds in his list that sold too few, too slowly. The list, as a whole, was not yet strong enough. It was certainly not rewarding him, financially, for all the time and energy he had put into it. Learned publishing—works of scholarship and advanced university textbooks—was dominated by the ancient University Presses and such discerning London firms as Macmillan and Longman. It was not, in any case, so remunerative in those days as the huge post-war expansion in student numbers and university libraries has since made it. As for general literature—fiction, biography, *belles lettres*—he could not, from Oxford, with little capital and a small sales organization, compete on level terms with the established publishers in London or the newcomers there, led by Cape, Faber, and Gollancz. He tried his hand at fiction, publishing Sylvia Thompson's first two novels and launching a series of 'Blackwell's 3s. 6d. Novels', but it would not do. A more successful enterprise was *The New Decameron*, a series of collections of short stories published at intervals from 1918 onwards. The contributors included A. E. Coppard, L. P. Hartley, D. H. Lawrence, Compton Mackenzie, V. Sackville-West, and Evelyn Waugh, 'some of the most notable names of the younger school of British authors', as the *Times Literary Supplement* reviewer approvingly remarked. The editor of the sixth 'day' (1930) was 'Vivienne Dayrell', who had worked as an assistant to Basil for years, and had, in 1927, become Mrs Graham Greene. Graham Greene himself had published his first book, *Babbling April*, with Blackwell in 1925.

The publication of Marten and Carter was a turning-point. Till then, B & M, as publishers, had been making a small loss each year, though they were able to set against this the modest profits of a binding firm that was absorbed into the company in the summer of 1922. But in 1926, the publishing business produced a profit (£900) and a dividend was declared for the first time. The company continued to grow steadily during the period covered by this chapter, and when the war broke out in 1939 a new subsidiary, Blackwell Scientific Publications, had just been formed.

This infant company owed its origin to the great Nuffield benefaction to the Oxford Medical School in 1936, and it was to specialize, and greatly prosper, in the field of medical publications. Its history belongs to later chapters, but Basil had already played some part, as an intermediary between gown and town, in the earliest benefaction to the University by Mr W. R. Morris, as he then was, in 1926. It was an odd story. L. R. Farnell, Rector of Exeter and from 1920 to 1923 Vice-Chancellor, wished to see a Chair of Spanish established in the University. He was a man of undeviating honesty and innocent tactlessness—Sir Michael Sadler once said of him 'If we had a pet hippopotamus we should be immensely proud of him but we should not welcome him in a china shop.' The good man hoped to get support for his pet project from Oxford's prosperous citizens, and Basil was consulted. How was he to approach Morris?

I recommended that he should do so through the Oxford Master Printer, publisher of *The Isis*, who had been a school fellow of Morris and called him by his Christian name, but Farnell saw otherwise, and wrote a letter to Alderman Sir Hugh Hall, the Conservative agent, I believe, in Oxford— I am told, in roughly these terms: 'This man Morris has done his best to wreck Oxford with his factory, and the least he could do would be to make a generous contribution to the University to whom his presence has been so prejudicial.' Sir Hugh Hall, with a tact equal only to that of Dr Farnell, forwarded the letter, just so, to Morris. I had the good fortune to see Morris's reply. It equalled in severity, and very nearly in dignity, Johnson's letter to Lord Chesterfield. It was a masterpiece of its kind, ending 'This is the first approach that has been made to me for support for a University undertaking. It will be the last.' But the situation was saved by the devotion of another Hall, Hall the Tailor, an old friend of Morris, who devoted some days when he should have been on holiday to waylaying and tackling Morris, and persuading him to a noble and generous reply—£10,000, in fact.[1]

As with all his subsequent benefactions, Morris gave wisely as well as generously. He felt that it was high time that Oxford paid more attention to modern studies, and he was interested in improving trade relations with Spain and South America. Thus was founded the King Alfonso XIII Chair of Spanish Studies in Oxford.

[1] Basil Blackwell.

X

The Bindery and other Outgrowths

I N the early years of the present century, there were several small binderies in Oxford, some of them dating back to the eighteenth century or even earlier, survivors from the days before books began to be issued in 'publisher's bindings'. Until the nineteenth century, books were normally sold by the publishers in folded sheets, the edges uncut, roughly stitched together and enclosed in paper covers. It was left to the customer to have his purchases bound according to his taste, and purse, and, of course, by hand. When the publishers began to issue every copy of an edition uniformly bound, machinery and mass production began to supersede handwork. An old-fashioned firm of half a dozen craftsmen, or less, working in one or two small rooms or attics, had neither the capital nor the space for elaborate machinery, but they were still needed for such 'one-off' jobs as book-repairing, binding up annual runs of periodicals, and fine binding in leather. The demand for these kinds of work was exceptionally high in Oxford, with its many libraries.

Benjamin Blackwell had gone into partnership with one of these firms, Ovenell and Fowles, as long ago as 1900. When Basil began to expand the publishing side in 1913, the connection with the bindery acquired added importance, and in 1922 it was wholly taken over and became an integral part of the newly incorporated firm of Blackwell and Mott. Ovenell and Fowles had by now outgrown their old premises in Wadham Place, Holywell, and it was time to move. There were some old coaching stables at No. 5 Alfred Street that might do. They were occupied by a section of Morris's motor manufactory, but the section was being moved to the new works at Cowley. Basil went to inspect. He found six men hammering away, making louvres in radiator bonnets. Morris named his price, Basil paid it, and Ovenell and Fowles moved in. No. 5 Alfred Street was later to become, for a time, the headquarters of Blackwell Scientific Publications, and then of B & M. Fowles was a character. He had been a notable amateur boxer in his young days, and did not suffer fools gently. Also, he liked to move with the times. He was proud of the mechanical 'gullotine', as he called it, bought second-hand, a bargain, a 'snip', some years earlier, and now he pulled off another snip by buying a second-hand Bremmer sewing machine for £50. The bindery prospered in its new quarters.

Another binding firm that had long been associated with Blackwell's was Morley Brothers, at 16 Longwall (now demolished to make room for the New College extension). In 1926, Morley's too became a subsidiary of Blackwell's, and proved a profitable investment. They specialized in fine binding for school and college prizes, as did another small firm who did work for Blackwell's, Hayes, of 5 Oriel Street, founded in 1730. A fourth bindery, W. T. Brown, whose speciality was account-book ruling and binding, occupied premises in Kemp Hall, off High Street. By 1937 all four of these binderies had been acquired by Blackwell, and after the war they were combined and moved to 33 St Aldate's to become the Kemp Hall Bindery.

The binding business came, in time, under the management of Geoffrey Barfoot. He had joined the firm in 1912 and caught Basil's attention by copying his device of a leaf to mark paragraphs. He thought him an observant youth with some energy and, deciding to cultivate him, drew him into the publishing unit. He writes:

He was one, and one of the best, to prove my dictum—with acknowledgement to Napoleon—that every novice in the firm has a director's fountain pen in his pocket. . . . One Saturday afternoon, I was in the course of making a certain proposal—to an entrancing maiden with the brightest of blue eyes and a pastel rose complexion which never faded—when my office door flew open and Geoffrey burst in; he took four eager steps in resounding boots, divined instantly that three were no company, reversed and departed without a word. Happily, a moment earlier, I had passed the point of no return and the dialogue was prosperously resumed. It was to continue blissfully for another sixty-three years.[1]

When Barfoot returned from his war service in France, he undertook clerical work for the Bindery, then known as Ovenell and Fowles, where his experience included dealing with primitive industrial relations. Basil remembers a breathless sheet-folding girl arriving with a message 'Could Mr Blackwell go at once—Mr Fowles is going to throw Mr Craddock out of the window.'

His competence grew with the growing business, until he finally retired as Manager of the new factory at Osney Mead and a Director of B & M. It was a great achievement.[2]

Much of it was due to his native wit, a capacity for hard work and an ability to work any machine better than the operative.

At the dinner given to him for fifty years of integrity, honesty, and devoted service, he made a speech which was both fascinating and moving. He traced his descent from peasant stock and described the funeral of his father who died when he was four. His mother, 'having exhausted the family exchequer on the funeral and burial of her mother just fourteen days before my father died was, after the purchase of a coffin for my father, forced to give him one of the last walking funerals in this city. The coffin was loaded outside the house on to a hand-cart and pushed through the streets with the mourners following on foot to the cemetery.'

It was characteristic of him that on this occasion he should look upon the dinner that was given to him not so much as thanks from the Company, but as an opportunity to say something himself: 'I cannot judge the quality of my own services that I have tried to give my master. It has been the best I have been capable of giving, but falls very short of paying the debt I owe him for his many and great kindnesses.'

Working hours were long in those days, but there were compensa-

---

[1] There are two versions of the story. Lady Blackwell used to maintain that she had only just brought Basil to the point of proposal and had to start all over again.
[2] Basil Blackwell.

GEOFFREY BARFOOT, 50 YEARS OF SERVICE
Richard   Basil   Geoffrey Barfoot   Julian

tions. The pressure of work varied in a stimulating way from week to week and from day to day. When there was a lull, the junior members of the staff found ways of letting off steam, all the more satisfactory because of the risk of detection. Tom Templeton, who joined in 1926, recalls some of their methods. 'At the end of the day, it was the apprentices' duty to take turns to carry the ledgers down to the front basement and stow them away in the great safe, and it was considered a great coup if one could lure one of the young ladies down there and shut her in the safe too, being careful of course not to leave her in there too long—or get caught in the process. This was but one of many similar competitions, another being the contest to see how high up the rungs of the ladder one could spring at a single jump. One of my own particular accomplishments was to hang head first down the spiral staircase, suspended by my feet from the top rail, one ill-timed performance scaring the wits out of an unfortunate customer on the way up.'

Life was, no doubt, hard on those who fell behind in the race, whether through innocent inability or wilful idleness, but that was accepted as the natural order of things. Accepted cheerfully, too, it seems. 'There was', Sir Basil recalls, 'a good deal of song to be heard in Blackwell's in the first third of this century. Hanks and Hunt sang in the choir at SS Phil and Jim, my father had a light alto, and I suppose if I had any voice at all it was a tenor. Assistants would sing at their work, and Hunt would run upstairs at the same time running up a scale. I do not know why this died out—partly, I think, because a certain solemnity due to our State educational system sub-dued the younger members of the staff. Apprentices used to be a pest for too lively conduct in their first year or two, letting off a certain amount of steam which later was devoted to sound book-selling. I believe the evil eleven-plus system brought anxiety into endless homes lest the boy or girl should fail in a crucial examination. Our apprentices became as solemn as sidesmen, and occasionally I would rebuke them for their gravity.' 'For the Boss, Mr Benjamin Henry', writes Barfoot, 'we all had a very wholesome respect. He treated us fairly and with kindness, though with a fair measure of firm and strict discipline. He had no use for knaves and people who were not prepared to work—and treated them as they deserved.' Everyone who worked in the Packing Department seems to have had diverting memories of old John Brain, 'a rather decrepit Dickensian character. The White Horse pub (next door) was in those days strictly "out of bounds" to all Blackwell employees, but old John liked his pint. Because of my affection for him, I did on many occasions keep "pike" for old John while he nipped into the White Horse for a very quick one. Beer in those days was 2*d*. per pint and that represented about the value in salary of 20 to 30 minutes work for a man.'

Barfoot recalls his first sight of the Boss's son. In January 1913, one day 'I was perched on my high stool at the long desk when through the low doorway (bending his head, necessary for a tall person) appeared a large athletic young man. Quickly I guessed this gentleman to be the new young Gaffer (Mr Basil) and so far forgot my humble position as to look round and stare. Uncle Bates at the next position on the long desk soon put me in place with a sharp rap on the knuckles with his ebony ruler.'

When Basil succeeded his father as head of the business in 1924, there had already been several other outgrowths from the centre in Broad Street, besides the binderies. There were warehouses in rented premises in Holywell and elsewhere to hold reserve stock for which there was no room in Broad Street. One of them, out at Blackhall Farm at the end of Charlbury Road, was only retained after 1924 on condition that the pensioner, Boyd, who kept an eye on it, lit a fire there 'more frequently' (but not, no doubt, too frequently, or enthusiastically). There was the charming little Octagon Bookshop at the corner of New College Lane, in the early sixteenth-century building that had once been the chapel of St. Mary the Virgin near Smythgate in the old City Wall. It displayed a selection of low-priced non-academic books, new and second-hand, prints and postcards, to attract the casual book-buyer and, in particular, the visitor to Oxford, and was presided over, in the twenties, by a Miss Hempel. It is alleged that one day, when a customer came seeking a second-hand Septuagint, she was at a loss, and asked for the name of the author. This shop had to be given up in 1923 when the Octagon was required by Hertford College to be incorporated in its new extension. Another small shop was then rented at 24 Holywell to serve the same purpose but that, too, was given up in 1930.

The Davenant Bookshop in Turl Street had a longer, and less unruffled, career. It was a dark old-fashioned Dickensian place, next to the Mitre Hotel, belonging to H. G. Gadney, a charming, cultivated but enigmatic man. In 1921, his business was in difficulties, and likely to be put on the market. After prolonged and complicated negotiations, it was acquired by Blackwell's in 1922, Gadney being left in charge as manager. But the poor man's eccentricities became more marked; there was a tragic breakdown which, despite efforts at restoration, rendered him incapable of performing the duties of manager and his employment was terminated. The shop was now renamed the Davenant Bookshop, and maintained a useful but not very remunerative existence until it underwent another metamorphosis in 1930. The Coverley Bookshop at 41 High Street had been offered to Blackwell by the proprietor, A. Graham, in 1928, and the stock was bought and the business taken over at the end of the year. In 1930, the Davenant Bookshop was transferred to 41 High Street, taking its name with it, and its old premises became the Turl Street Cash Bookshop. Blackwell gave up the High Street shop when the lease expired in 1938, but the Turl Street shop justified itself, mainly as an outlet for remainders and second-hand books which could not afford the cost of cataloguing or of shelf-space in Broad Street. It was Naboth's vineyard to the Mitre Hotel which it adjoined. Lincoln College was the landlord of both, and when the lease was due to be renewed the Bursar told Basil that the Hotel had made an attractive offer to rent 2–3 Turl Street with the design of extending their restaurant; he did not think that the trade of the bookshop would enable it to match the Mitre's offer. Basil agreed, but said he would be sorry to lose the tenancy, for his grandfather was the occupying tenant at the time of his death in 1855. The Bursar, with singular humanity, replied 'Oh, then, we should not wish to disturb you.' In 1976, the old building was condemned as unsafe and had to be vacated for future demolition and reconstruction as a part of the plan for the extension of the College.

At the end of our present period, Basil became involved in rescue operations on the other side of Broad Street. The story of his connection with Parker's is best told in his own words.

In 1879, and for many years after, Parker's in the Broad was the dominant bookshop in Oxford. The Parker family, deriving from Samuel Parker, Bishop of Oxford, President of Magdalen and the King's agent in the famous resistance of the Fellows to the interference of James II, established the tradition of gentlemen booksellers in Oxford. The memory of Sackville Parker, the Bishop's grandson, is preserved by Boswell in Johnson's tender tribute to him after his visit to his shop at the corner of Logic Lane in 1784. His bookseller nephew Joseph, a most effective partner with the University in the Bible Press and agent for the books on the 'Learned side', was succeeded in 1832 by his nephew John Henry Parker, scholar and antiquary, who as a bookseller and publisher of Keble, Pusey, and others of the Oxford Movement, of the *Library of the Fathers*, the *Library of Anglo-Catholic Theology* and the *Oxford Pocket Classics*, was for half a century the outstanding figure in the Oxford world of letters.

Friend of Gladstone, Hon. MA, and CB, he died full of years in 1884. Under his son James bookselling became predominant, publishing activities dwindled, and the Agency for the University Press came to an end.

James Parker was to become an Oxford figure hardly less distinguished than his father. Scholar and antiquary, in his turn he was to win recognition and an Hon. MA for his services to Archaeology and Liturgical studies. He was succeeded at his death in 1912 by his son Charles.

When he had finished his University studies and entered the family business Charles was, I fancy, a lonely and uncertain young man, not ready like his forebearers to bestride the two communities civic and academic, but somewhat remote from both. He retreated with his wife to a dignified old house some three miles from Oxford, where they bred St. Bernard dogs. There were no children, and they saw little company. Occasionally, I would visit him there, having a liking for him, for behind his farouche manner, loud voice, and defensive monocle there was a generous spirit which emerged in quiet conversation. In the course of one of these talks towards the end of his life he asked me 'to do my best for the business if anything should happen to him'. I gave my promise.

After his death in 1930, the business was carried on for a few years as a private limited company, but in 1937 the trustees advertised it for sale. The two working directors, John Powell and Will Thomas, were eager to preserve its identity; between them they were able to raise half the sum required, and I undertook that the balance should be provided from the other side of Broad Street on condition that there should be no interference in their conduct of the business, and that Parker's and Blackwell's should remain in amiable competition. Will Hunt and Harry Critchley joined the Board, and it was for me as Chairman to hold the balance. The arrangement worked happily as it does today.[1]

Parker's remained on its historic site at the corner of Turl Street and Broad Street, though it lost its upper floor, long a happy hunting-ground for second-hand bargains, and had to put on a new face, when Exeter College built a new extension at the north-west corner of its territory in the sixties. Just before the 1939–45 war, a similar sacrifice to progress threatened the south frontage of Broad Street from the opposite corner of Turl Street westward. The land belonged to the City, leases were soon to fall in, and a plan was

[1] Basil Blackwell.

afoot to replace the irregular row of old houses with a tidy, efficient, and more profitable cliff of up-to-date architecture. The old-established bookselling firm of Joseph Thornton and Son, and F. A. Wood, who combined bookselling with stationery, were alarmed, and took separate counsel with Blackwell. Wood was eventually taken over, but happily the City's plan came to nothing and Thornton's survived.

A new growth that was to bear much fruit in the future took place far away from Oxford. In 1927, the well-known Bristol firm of William George and Sons was in danger of going out of business. A granddaughter, dutifully helping her elderly father, was now the mainstay of the family business, and a clergyman had asked her to marry him. She had met Basil at the Booksellers' Conference that year, and came to consult him.

We examined various expedients of which the most profitable, as it seemed to me, would be to sell the freehold to a thriving draper, maybe, and let the stock go for what it might fetch. Such a prospect distressed her, and in the end we arranged that Blackwell's should be responsible for the conduct of the business and that the George family should have a substantial interest as sleeping partners. It has proved a happy arrangement.[1]

Happy indeed. The business revived and Miss George was able to marry her clergyman.

The shop, in Park Street, was near the young university whose growth was being so generously fostered by the Wills family. Working parties from Oxford brought new life and expertise into the business, and improvements were made in the premises—five tons of unsaleable second-hand stock were cleared out in the first few months—and by 1938 Blackwell was able to announce that the business had 'all the appearance of a sound investment'. When he took charge the annual turnover was £8,000. Fifty years later it had multiplied more than a hundredfold.

[1] Basil Blackwell.

XI

External Affairs: 1924–1939

BASIL had had to carry an increasingly heavy load when his father's vigour began to decline in his last years. After his death, the pressure grew still greater, for he became wholly responsible, as Chairman, for the bookselling business as well as for his young publishing firm. 'I never worked so hard again' he has said. But he was supported by colleagues in Broad Street in whose ability, experience, and loyalty he had complete confidence, and in 1925 he made a short break by paying his first, and only, visit to the United States. He went to promote the export not only of books in general and of his own publications in particular, but of the fine bindings that were the speciality of the Oxford binderies. The short spell of a different kind of hard work refreshed him, but his commitments grew steadily. By 1929, at the age of forty, he was one of the most flourishing booksellers in the country, and the most influential. He was consulted on trade matters by publishers as well as booksellers and his views carried the more weight because he was a member of both groups.

In 1925 and 1926, he served as President of the Antiquarian Booksellers' Association, an office which his father had held twelve years earlier. Benjamin Henry, as we have seen, started out as an antiquarian bookseller, with new books as a second string. Though the position was soon reversed, the sale of antiquarian books continued to be a vital element in the business, not only on its own account, but because of the contacts it set up. A university librarian who found that Blackwell's admirable antiquarian catalogues helped him to fill gaps in his existing collections might well be led to buy his new books from the same source. The Founder continued in personal

charge of the Antiquarian Department until his death. William King
(of whose character and career something will be told in Chapter
XIII) was then put in charge of it and asked to make suggestions for
its development. This brings us to the story of Basil and 'The Ring'.

Traditionally [he writes] our secondhand stock was maintained by the
purchase of lots large or small offered for sale by current customers or by
their executors. I had suggested to my father that we should fortify the
stock by some constructive buying at auction. 'That is out of the question,' he replied, 'The Ring would run us off any lot for which we might
bid, unless we joined them, and we must not do that.' He explained what
was meant by 'The Ring'; booksellers attending an auction would agree
not to bid against each other in the room; one, or perhaps two, of them
would bid on behalf of them all, for lack of competition the winning
bids were low, and the books might be bought for prices well below their
current value. Later the group would meet and hold an informal auction
among themselves at which the books would fetch competitive prices,
and then the difference between the aggregate paid in the auction room
and in the subsequent 'settlement' would be shared among the members
of the Ring. This difference would be so substantial that the Ring's buyer
could afford to outbid any competitor for an isolated item (or force him
to pay more than the book's worth), recovering any excess from the
surplus to be shared. True enough; but the weapon is two-edged and any
individual, if he have sufficient knowledge, may force up the price of any
and every lot to the limit of profitable purchase leaving the last bid, but
no profit, to the Ring. I had resolved after my father's death to make
such an example in order that our confrères in the antiquarian trade might
be aware that we would take no part in the Ring, that we were content
to compete on reasonable terms for such books as we might wish to
acquire, and not to bid for others unless there were evidence of an inten-
tion to set against us.

The catalogue of an important auction sale appeared soon after
King's appointment. Basil told him to go through it, lot by lot,
marking against each the top market price, and then a tough
assistant, unknown in 'the rooms', went to the sale and bid up to
that price for every item. He did not get the books, for the Ring
bid too, but they had to pay the top price, or a bit more, for every
lot. Once was enough. They never tried again to force Blackwell's

man out of the bidding. The Antiquarian Booksellers' Association did not, of course, recognize the Ring, though their rules did not specifically condemn it. But their new President had made his own position clear. He was jealous of the Trade's reputation for fair dealing, and soon found occasion to uphold it practically, though privately, in 1926. Blackwell's had sent a first edition of *Alice in Wonderland* for sale by auction in London. It had been bought for £40, which according to 'Book Auction Records' had seemed a fair price at the time. To his surprise it fetched £330 in the saleroom, and this was announced on the BBC that night. The doors were barely open the next morning before a little old lady, she who had sold the book, was asking to see Mr Blackwell. She admitted she had accepted his offer, but it did seem a bit hard . . . Basil cut her short by asking if she had left her house before the postman called that morning. She said she had. He suggested she should go back and see if the postman had brought a letter with an enclosure from the firm (a cheque for £100), and he heard no more.

Collusive bidding at auction is difficult to define with effective precision and hard to prevent. Lord Darling's Act of 1927 did not succeed in stopping it, but after the second war the practice began to attract uncomfortable publicity and questions in the House of Commons. Blackwell again intervened and the ABA made a new Rule, that any member who should contravene the Auctions (Bidding Agreements) Act should, whether legally convicted or not, be asked to resign from the Association. The snake is now scotched, if not killed.

Benjamin Blackwell had served for many years on the Council of the Associated Booksellers (BA for short hereafter) and only failing health prevented his becoming President in the early twenties. After his death, his son succeeded him on the Council and was President from 1934 to 1936 (and Basil's sons Richard, thirty years later, and Julian in 1980). When Basil came on to the Council the book trade as a whole was in a bad way. The publishers, it is true, were doing well enough, but the lot of many booksellers was little happier than a century earlier, when the bibliographer, T. F. Dibdin, published his *Remarks on the Present Languid and Depressed State of*

Literature and the Book Trade. Basil himself was by no means languid or depressed, but he well understood the plight of many of his fellow bookmen, and worked hard and unselfishly to rescue them. In 1931, he was invited to give the first of the J. M. Dent Memorial Lectures in Stationers' Hall. *The World of Books*, as he called his lecture (published in 1932) was a memorable survey of the functions of author, printer, publisher, and bookseller, a characteristic blend of uplift and admonition.

In order to live in the World of Books, it is necessary to live in the World of Men, and the Bookman's ideals must be amenable to economics. We shall do well then to consider how far the Book World is economically organised and whether, and where, there is room for improvement without hampering that individualism which is its soul. Booksellers as a whole are unworldly people, and both they and the Book Trade suffer for it, in that far too many allow themselves to be caught in a web of detail. Their minds are cumbered about with the minutiae of routine when they should be addressed to the problem of constructive selling . . . they are too busy to think.

But better organization of the trade as a whole and improved business methods in the individual bookshop were not enough.

The way to prosperity . . . lies through an increased reading public. . . . I can imagine no more valuable service to all the partners in the Book Trade than the adoption by publishers of a sane and scientific method of cooperative advertisement directed at the *unreading* public.

But it was uphill work for the statesmen of the book world like Blackwell and Stanley Unwin. Individualism may have been the soul of the book trade, but it was possible to be too soulful. It was, of course, a natural trait. Books are unlike any other kind of merchandise. They are not 'absolutely dead things', as Milton remarked, but have a life of their own, and even a sort of power of reproduction. You can never tell how they will behave. Consider the story of the *Oxford English Dictionary*, divertingly described in the pages of Peter Sutcliffe's *Informal History of the Oxford University Press* published to celebrate the quincentenary of the Press in 1978. When the Delegates agreed, a hundred years ago, to take in hand a New

English Dictionary on Historical Principles, the Philological Society, which had spent twenty years collecting materials, estimated that the work would run to 7,000 pages and would be completed in ten years. They were sure that it would be 'wonderfully remunerative'. The Delegates were at any rate cautious on the last point, and would not go further than 'express a confident expectation that if the profits proved higher than expected their successors would entertain favourably any application put to them by the Society'. In the event the work ran to over 16,000 pages, took fifty years to complete, and left them with a loss of nearly £400,000. But another surprise was to come. The bread cast so benevolently but ignorantly upon the Victorian waters was to be found again, most abundantly, after many days. The great Dictionary's offspring, Shorter, Concise, Pocket, and so on, were to repay their progenitor's losses many times over.

Such unpredictabilities bring colour into the lives of bookmen and keep their spirits up—and nourish their objections to being told what to do, and how to do it. But the problems of the British book trade in the twenties were too serious to allow everyone to be a law unto himself. Publishers, booksellers, and authors had to be persuaded to appreciate the need for greater cooperation. It was actually an author, Hugh Walpole, who inaugurated the process. He had established his own reputation, on both sides of the Atlantic, as a successful novelist and a very popular, and well-paid, lecturer, and had no personal axe to grind, but he had the interests of literature in general at heart. He saw the need to overcome what Michael Sadleir, in his article on Walpole in the *Dictionary of National Biography*, calls the 'obstinate individualisms of the various branches of the book trade', and in an address to a literary club in 1920 he appealed to all bookmen to get together. The Society of Bookmen 'for the advancement of literature' came into being in 1921 with Walpole as its first president.

The Society was an unofficial body whose members, though drawn, purposely, from all parts of the World of Books, represented no one but themselves. There were at the outset about fifty members, among them Basil Blackwell. The most active and influential of the publishers was Stanley Unwin, and it was on his initiative that the National Book Council came into being in 1925, an official body representing and supported by the trade associations.

One of the most fruitful results of the deliberations of the Society of Bookmen was the Book Tokens scheme. The brainchild of a publisher, Harold Raymond of Chatto and Windus, it was discussed by the Society, and recommended to the NBC in 1928, though it was not until 1932 that the ingenious eloquence of Blackwell at the Booksellers' annual conference at Chester persuaded the trade to put this novel, and therefore suspect, idea into practice. Perhaps, too, in the aftermath of the slump, they felt ready to try anything. 'Do you know', he said, 'how many (though he himself had no idea how many) thousands of postal orders are never cashed by the careless public? It will be the same with these Tokens. The scheme is sure to make a profit.' He got his way, and the scheme was launched in time for the Christmas season that same year, despite the refusal of many booksellers to cooperate. The public gratefully welcomed this convenient solution of their Christmas present problems, to say nothing of birthdays and other occasions. Book tokens had come to stay, and have proved an even greater blessing half a century later, when soaring postal rates have discouraged us all from sending parcels. There were some difficulties behind the scenes at first. As Blackwell had truly predicted, more and more tokens were not redeemed and the question of what to do with the growing hoard, held by a Book Tokens Committee set up as a central clearing house, led to much argument, and some ill-feeling, between the BA, the NBC, and the PA. Blackwell again came to the rescue, in 1935, as President of the BA, and agreement was finally reached under his persuasive chairmanship. The scheme grew and prospered—within ten years over a million tokens were being sold each year—and when, in 1943, it was decided, for tax reasons, to form a limited company to administer the scheme, another public-spirited champion from Blackwell's, Henry Schollick, served as its first chairman for twenty-five years. His entry into Blackwell's is related in the next chapter.

It was a happy chance that Stanley Unwin was President of the PA when Basil Blackwell became President of the B.A. They were old friends and like-minded in their concern for the welfare of the trade. The informal partnership—they were in the habit of lunching together once a fortnight—produced a great and lasting improvement in the relations between the two groups. Another old friend, Humphrey Milford, who had been President of the PA from 1919 to 1921, paid his warm tribute to the retiring President of the BA in a letter from Amen House, then the London office of the OUP, on 15 May 1936:

My Dear Blackwell

Now that 'home you've gone', and the only 'wages' there are likely to be are the respect and affection of your colleagues, I felt that I should like to add the feeble plaudits of a mere onlooker to the far more intimate and valuable tributes of your fellow-members. May I say, therefore, that I have admired immensely your conduct of your important and difficult office; that I consider that in your two years you have done a great deal to bring the two associations more closely together; and that if a succession of Presidents like yourself were conceivable, I should not even despair of the eventual formation of a joint board to look after the interests of both branches of the trade.

Yours ever
Humphrey Milford

And now perhaps you will have leisure to propose yourself to lunch here one day instead of creeping through the Square disguised in cloak and sombrero!

It had been very hard work, and Basil himself told his colleagues at Oxford that 'the happiest day in the year was that on which I ceased to be first officer of the Associated Booksellers of Great Britain and Ireland, and so became able to devote more time to affairs in Broad Street'. A striking example of his imaginative wisdom had been his invitation to Unwin to be joint host to an informal week-end conference of fifty publishers and booksellers at Ripon Hall in Oxford in 1934. The theme set by Blackwell for general discussion was 'The New Reading Public'. One of the publishers was a young man of thirty-two from the Bodley Head, Allen Lane. He already had in his mind the idea of cheap paperback reprints of copyright books. In 1935 he launched Penguin Books.

1. Ernest Barker (Chester). 2. Lovat Dickson (later Macmillan). 3. E. V. Rieu (Methuen; Penguin). 4. Geoffrey Bles (later Collins). 5. John Hampden (Nelson). 6. W. A. R. Collins (later Sir William). 7. Will Hunt (Blackwell). 8. ? 9. Lindsey Drummond. 10. ? Driver (C.U.P.). 11. R. F. West (Baillière Tyndall and Cox). 12. Cadness Page (Harrods). 13. John Murray (John Murray). 14. ? Richardson (Harrods). 15. F. Crawley (Faber). 16. J. R. Laing (Blackie). 17. F. Melcher (U.S. Pub. Weekly). 18. Frank Sanders (Pub. Assoc.). 19. K. Potter (Longman). 20. Allen Lane (Penguin). 21. Sir Adrian Mott (Blackwell). 22. ? Simpson (Golder, Reading). 23. John Grant (Blackwell). 24. ? 25. G. Wren Howard (Cape). 26. ? 27. Charles Sisson. 28. C. W. Cragg (Students' Bookshop). 29. A. F. Mason (Worthing). 30. F. S. Thornton (Oxford). 31. 'Wilson of Bumpus'. 32. J. Le Tahl (Bath). 33. H. E. Alden (Slatter and Rose). 34. Miss H. M. Light (Booksellers Assoc.). 35. Garfield Hull. 36. Eleanor Halliday. 37. B. Christian (Nisbet). 38. G. B. Bowes (Cambridge). 39. Sir Stanley Unwin (Allen & Unwin). 40. Basil Blackwell (Blackwell). 41. Harold Raymond (Chatto). 42. Ainslie Thin (James Thin). 43. E. W. Heffer (Cambridge). 44. G. Anderson (Harrap). 45. G. W. Taylor (Dent). 46. H. L. Jackson (Lewis). 47. Esmond Morgan (Newcastle). 48. ? Stewart (Faber). 49. Maurice Hockliffe (Bedford). 50. Hubert Wilson (London). 51. Henry Schollick (Blackwell). 52. Alan S. Jackson (Glasgow). 53. C. E. Pearce (Overs, Rugby).

RIPON HALL CONFERENCE, 1934

We are now so accustomed to paperbacks that it is hard to recall, and for the younger generation to imagine, what the book scene was like before Penguins appeared on the stage. Even the cheapest reprint series, Nelson's red 'sevenpennies', so popular in the early years of the century, were cloth-bound; and 7*d*. was a great deal more in 1906 than 6*d*. in 1936. By then nothing of the kind cost less than 2*s*. For paperbacks of contemporary authors, you had to go abroad. Tauchnitz of Leipzig had launched their celebrated continental series in 1841 (the 1939 war put an end to them), but they could only be bought on the other side of the Channel. They were travelling companions for the Englishman abroad, cheap (the equivalent of one shilling or less) and pocketable, but contraband when he recrossed the Channel—though a good many were slipped through the customs at Dover and Newhaven by forgetful or, like Miss Amy Frush in Henry James's *The Third Person*, deliberately daring travellers.

At home, then, hardbacks were the rule. It was no use, surely, to try to change this well-established tradition. Sir William Williams,[1] in *Allen Lane: A Personal Portrait*, records that when Jonathan Cape was approached by Lane to allow some of his books to appear as Penguins, he remarked, 'If he wants paperback rights of some of my titles why shouldn't I take his money off him? I know he'll fail.' He would, it seems, have thought twice about it if there had been any question of Lane succeeding. As for the booksellers, they saw no profit in selling books at sixpence, and they gave Lane no encouragement. But Woolworth's, whose standard price was then sixpence, came to the rescue with large orders, and repeat orders, and soon Penguins were finding their way into every bookshop. What had been thought to be a threat to the trade, though an empty one, turned out to be a by no means empty blessing. Lane had paid the public the compliment of believing that it was the best books that they wanted cheap, not trash, and he was right. What is more, the popularity of his Penguins was infectious, and stimulated the demand for books in general.

[1] Sir William (Emrys) Williams (1896–1977), chief editor and director of Penguin 1935–65; founder member of the Arts Council, and Secretary-General 1951–63.

In the twenties the English were buying fewer books per head of the population than the New Zealanders or the Scots. An increased reading public, as Blackwell said in his Dent lecture, would be the best tonic for the ailments of the book trade. Book Tokens and Penguins were to bring many more people into the bookshops, but the booksellers needed not only more customers but better organization and more up-to-date business methods. At Blackwell's, it is true, turnover doubled between 1924 and 1939, but the profit margin fell. Most booksellers were finding it hard to make ends meet and some were going out of business. When Basil became President of the BA he initiated an independent enquiry into the economics of the trade. The accounts of twenty representative booksellers, large and small, were analysed by a chartered accountant, R. W. Thornton, and he submitted his report to the annual meeting of the BA in 1935. It revealed a state of affairs that Thornton described as 'almost appalling'. On an average turnover of £17,000, producing an average gross profit of £5,000, the net profit, after deducting overhead expenses of £4,000, interest on capital, and a very modest rate of remuneration for directors and proprietors, amounted to £71! This average meant of course that some booksellers were losing money. There was no getting away from these gloomy figures. Thornton carried out a more detailed survey over a wider field in the following year which only served to confirm them. They became a useful weapon in discussions with the publishers about trade terms.

The newspaper proprietors' circulation war, referred to above in the account of the Shakespeare Head Press, was at its height when Basil became President of the BA. Their offers to their subscribers of cut-price sets of Dickens and other non-copyright authors were a serious enough threat to the booksellers, but when it began to look as if living authors were going to favour the same treatment for *their* works, Basil went into action. Bernard Shaw was the offender:

Dear Mr. Shaw,   October 23rd, 1934

When Constable & Co. published 'The Complete Plays of Bernard Shaw' at 12s. 6d. net, they assured the Trade that there would be no reprint. This statement was freely used by booksellers in selling the book to their customers.

The publication of 'The Complete Plays of Bernard Shaw' by Odhams Press for sale solely to subscribers to *The Daily Herald* (at 3s. 9d., plus six tokens) has placed those booksellers in the unfortunate position of having deceived the public.

It must be admitted that the new edition differs from the 'Complete Edition' in containing three more plays (though this is small consolation original purchasers); but apart from these extra pages and the *Warning from the Author*, apparently the new edition is in fact a reprint from the plates of Constable's edition.

I can hardly suppose that Constable gave the booksellers their assurance without your consent. It would help those booksellers (already sufficiently penalised) who are charged by their customers with a breach of faith, if you could arm them with a statement exonerating them from complicity.

Yours sincerely,

Basil Blackwell

25th October 1934

Dear Basil Blackwell

In future, when a customer asks you for a book of mine, say 'Thanks very much', wrap the book up nicely in paper for him (or her), take the money, give the change, say 'Thanks very much' over again, and bow the customer out.

If, out of pure gratuitous incontinence you prefer to enter into conversation and give unsolicited assurances, of an obviously idiotic character, about my business intentions, you do it at your own risk; and if it turns out subsequently that I never had any such intentions you will have to exhonerate [*sic*] yourself as best you can.

I have given Constables a letter to the effect that they took no part in The Daily Herald transaction except to oppose it with all their might. I can do nothing for the booksellers but tell them not to be childish.

In America I have lately had two orders of 50,000 copies each from Book Clubs, to be given away to their members *for nothing*, as a bonus. Of course I accepted both.

I am looking forward to an order from Woolworths for a sixpenny edition.

Would you, Basil, refuse such business if it came your way?

And have you no bowels of compassion for the millions of your fellow countrymen who can no more afford a twelve and sixpenny book than a trip round the world. You should see some of their letters.

I am really surprised at you. When we met at Bumpus's, you seemed quite an intelligent youth.

Faithfully
G. Bernard Shaw

29th October, 1934

Tush and fie! Mr. Shaw, you evade.

I must enlist the aid of our other Omnibus playwright in recalling the Lord Chief Justice's words to Falstaff:—

'Sir John, Sir John, I am well acquainted with your manner of wrenching the true cause the false way. It is not a confident brow, nor the throng of words that come with such more than impudent sauciness from you, can thrust me from a level consideration.'

My 'level consideration' is that Constable's edition of 'THE COMPLETE PLAYS' was sold to the booksellers, and by the booksellers to the Public on the assurance that there would not be a reprint; that this assurance ('idiotic' perhaps, but neither invented nor suggested by the booksellers) was given with your knowledge and consent; that later, according to your letter, business opportunity jumping with your generous impulses, you authorised a reprint; that this practice leaves you with the halfpence, your publishers and the booksellers with the kicks.

'You speak as having power to do wrong; but answer in the effect of your reputation.'

Yours sincerely,
Basil Blackwell

The episode recalls Benjamin Henry Blackwell's encounter with Hilaire Belloc thirty years earlier. As then, the last word was with a Blackwell. When the three letters were printed, at Shaw's own request, in the *Publishers Circular*, R. W. Chapman sent Basil a postcard: 'BB v GB α+'. A few months later the SHP *Shakespeare* was published, and 50,000 copies were sold in no time. This was too much for the newspaper proprietors. The other trade journal, the

Bookseller, acclaimed the President's stout attack on their 'marauding practice' and predicted, correctly, that 'this newspaper nuisance will abate'.

Basil's concern for the welfare of the trade, his approachability, and his enthusiasm endeared him to his fellow booksellers. His nickname the 'Gaffer', already in use in Broad Street since 1924, and not unknown outside, was publicly affixed to him at the Book-sellers' Banquet at Newcastle in 1935. John Newsom,[1] an intimate friend of the family for many years, rose unbidden from his chair at the end of the dinner and 'irreverently and out of order called on the company to drink the health of the Gaffer'. The name stuck.

[1] Sir John Newsom, Chief Education Officer Hertfordshire 1940–57. Joined Long-man's in 1957 and subsequently became a Director of the Longman Group. He was Chairman of the committee set up by the Central Advisory Council for Education which produced the report 'Half our Future'.

XII

Changes in Broad Street
1924–1939

'FORTY years ago', the Chairman told the shareholders of BHB at the Annual General Meeting in 1937, 'my father was dissuaded from approaching the Trustees of the Churchmen's Union buildings with an offer to buy the freehold, by his brother-in-law, who said that sooner or later the property was bound to be offered for sale by the Trustees, the price would then be lower, and that as the firm of Morrell Peel and Gamlen, with whom he was, acted for the Trustees he would know when they wished to sell. The event proved that this was the one thing he did not know; and one day my father found that Trinity College had acquired the freehold. This I believe to be the only serious mistake my father made in business.'

The consequences of the mistake were severe. For many years, Blackwell's continued to occupy the buildings as tenants of Trinity, and even when, in 1922, the College demolished one of the two Union Rooms ('Ultima Thule') to make room for their War Memorial Library, its basement was eventually leased to Blackwell's, and provided space for some 30,000 books. But the possibility of erecting a large new building on the site was lost. The only alternative was to expand eastwards, along the Broad, but Trinity also owned 49 and 48, next door, and Bliss Court.

By the time that he had succeeded his father, Basil had struck up a close friendship with the redoubtable President of Trinity, Dr Blakiston. 'Blinks' as all Trinity men, and some outside the college, called him, loved to bathe in the nude, and this he was able to do in the secluded swimming pool at Osse Field, Basil's home at Appleton. There, with the minimum of formality, the two friends discussed men and books—and buildings. The old President sympathized with the young Bookseller in his need for more space and Basil hopefully laid plans for rebuilding on Trinity land. At the end of 1930, encouraged by Dr Blakiston, he made the college an offer of £5,000 for the freehold of 48 and 49 and Bliss Court, but the Governing Body, by a majority of one, turned it down, much to the President's annoyance. Instead, they offered to buy the freehold of 50 and 51, and to negotiate a building lease on the rest. This, of course, was out of the question, and the onset of the depression 'stopped play'. Some extra elbow-room was provided by a space-saving reconstruction of No. 50 which produced the Jubilee Room (1933), to celebrate the firm's fiftieth birthday in 1929, but the pressure remained and grew.

Meanwhile the University was planning the new Bodleian, and in 1936 the charming old houses east of No. 48 to the corner of Parks Road were demolished to make room for Sir Giles Gilbert Scott's massive new building. The clearing of the site and the deep excavations needed to house three of the eleven floors of the book-stands underground shook Nos. 48 and 49 literally to their foundations, and they were scheduled as a dangerous building. Something had to be done, and negotiations with Trinity were reopened. This time the deadlock was broken. The College still had its eyes on the freehold of 50 and 51, but now only asked for an option to buy if Blackwell's ever wanted to sell, a contingency that Basil was content to regard as remote. On this condition, Trinity agreed to grant a building lease of the site of 48, 49, and Bliss Court, at an annual rent of £155, for eighty years. Things began to move quickly. The plans were passed by the Corporation, the last of the old ladies in Bliss Court were found accommodation elsewhere, B & M's publishing offices were transferred to Alfred Street for the duration of building operations, and the work began. It was completed on 30 September 1938, the day when Chamberlain came back from Munich proclaiming 'peace in our time'. It had been a bold decision to invest in the future when the future looked so bleak, but Basil's faith was to be

NEW BUILDINGS

well justified. The decision was taken only just in time. A year later, and the project would have had to be deferred until after the war, and would have cost two or three times as much.

The Chairman and his fellow directors had watched the new building take shape with relief but also with some misgivings. For one thing, it had to pay for itself. The loan from the bank must be repaid, and there would be some increase in overheads, but the extra space and the improved layout of the whole of the shop and offices were planned to produce more business and higher profits, and would surely do so. There were, however, other considerations, as Basil wrote in the 'Note on the New Buildings' circulated to customers and colleagues in the trade. 'We were loath to disturb the old rambling shop which had grown through the years by a series of makeshift measures, and with which a number of us had grown. . . . Design in a bookshop, as in a garden, can hardly yield the charm of casual development.' True, but the fact was that for customers and staff alike charm had for long been paid for by increasing congestion and inconvenience. Novelty, in moderation, has its own charms, and there was no denying its utility. The seeker after foreign books, for example, did not complain that they were now all efficiently concentrated in one room instead of dispersed in several; and it was the same in the other main departments. Once you had got your new bearings, you could find what you wanted more easily and more quickly. There was a children's room too, and one where teachers could examine the latest schoolbooks. But the rapid growth of the business after the war made still more expansion necessary. There have been notable additions to the 1938 buildings in the last twenty years, in which, again, the plans of the bookshop and of Trinity have had to be coordinated.

The directors who were responsible for the new buildings were those same who had been appointed by the Founder when the Company was formed in 1920, and three of them had come to Blackwell's while Queen Victoria was still on the throne. One of the 'Pillars of the House', Fred Hanks, had celebrated his jubilee in 1933. The University marked the occasion by conferring on him the degree of Master of Arts *honoris causa*, in recognition of his service in 'one of the most pleasant of the unofficial departments of the University'. William ('Rhino') Hunt, the second Pillar and, like Hanks, a director since 1920, would have celebrated his jubilee in 1939, but it was not to be. Towards the end of 1938, he began to lose the sight of his right eye, cancer was diagnosed, and in the following January he died. The loss of this modest, vigorous, and most loyal of men was deeply felt in Broad Street and also by a wide circle of friends and colleagues in the trade. For more than thirty years, he had been responsible for the buying of new books from the publishers, and a visit to 'Mr Hunt' was one of the most important events in a representative's journeys; thrice a year the 'reps' called in those days, the grave seniors among them still wearing morning dress. The *Bookseller* recorded that Hunt 'never spared himself in his work for the [Booksellers'] Association by means of which he hoped to raise the standing of the book trade, and to improve the conditions of his fellow booksellers'. He served as Secretary and later Chairman of the Oxford branch, and he sat on the Council of the Association in London for many years. In his tribute to him, published in *The Bookseller*, the following lines appeared written by the Gaffer:

> Oh loyal heart farewell!
> How much I dare not tell
> Of me is lost with you
> Who my life through
> As colleague friend and guide
> Stood at my side.
>
> How humble was my heart
> To hear you praise my part,
> Who was the indebted one,
> In glad days gone
> Thoughtful in your distress
> To thank and bless.
>
> You made our leave-taking
> A lovely thing
> So, for all thanks I gave
> In life, still at your grave
> Your debtor I—
> You taught me how to die.

Charles Field, the third of the founding directors who had joined the firm before the turn of the century, only missed his jubilee by a few years when he died in 1942. He had a devoted disciple in Frank Timbs, who came to Broad Street as a small boy in 1925, at 7s. 6d. a week, of which his mother took 7s.

Even in those days my 6d. didn't go far. My duties were to enter in a small black book the names and addresses and postage on all the parcels, stick stamps on and struggle with them to the Post Office a little way down the road. . . . To buy stamps for the parcels I was given a piece of cardboard on which was written '£3 for stamps please'. This token was inserted into one of the mechanical miracles of the age; I can only describe it as a wooden tube which went vertically from the shop through the floor of the room above. In the square tube was a miniature 'lift' measuring about 5 in. by 2. The cardboard was placed in this lift and the bottom of the tube given a sharp kick, whereupon an unknown deity hauled away to the cashier's office. In a while, the little box would thud to the bottom and lo! there were three one-pound notes, or two months' wages!

After a while . . . I was given the job of office boy . . . The staff in the office at that time consisted of Mr C. W. Field, Mr C. W. Cutler, Mr F. W. Cox (known as Horace), Miss Irene Quartermain (Bussie) a typist, Miss 'Paddy' Coombes, and the boy . . . My chief duties were to put into alphabetical order the day's invoices and answer the company telephone (Oxford 217). We had one line, one instrument, and a switch on the wall to put calls through to Blackwell and Mott who shared our number.

When Hunt died in January 1939, the Company was left with no director to represent it on the Council of the Booksellers' Association, and a new director was appointed for this purpose and to undertake 'other special duties that might be allocated to him'. The new director was Henry Lightbown Schollick, and special duties in plenty were ahead of him. He had been engaged by Basil in 1932 to lend a hand on the publishing side, whose rapid growth required guidance and nurture. At the AGM of B & M at the end of that year, the Chairman described him as 'a very able and industrious young man, who relieved me more and more of an almost insupportable burden'. Henry Schollick, 'Uncle Henry' as he became, not only in Oxford but throughout the book trade, as the years matured his wisdom and affability, was a Lancashire man, born in 1906, who had come up from Blackburn Grammar School to Oriel, as a scholar of the college, and began his business career in a multiple store in Glasgow. He moved from there to the publishing firm of Collins, but soon found something not congenial in his work, and it was a lucky day for Blackwell's when he applied for a post, and was appointed. He came on three months' probation, but there is no record of the appointment ever having been confirmed.

H.L.S. learned his trade quickly and thoroughly. A colleague remembered him 'travelling' the booksellers in Tabitha ('full of good works'), his Austin Seven of a late 1920 vintage, making lasting friendships up and down the country. When E. W. Parker, who had also come from Collins to Blackwell's, died in 1933, he succeeded him as a director of B & M and he became the chief architect of the Company's further expansion. Two years later, he saved his firm from incineration. 'A visitor', writes James Sherbourn, 'had thrown a smouldering match or cigarette end into H.L.S.'s large, almost full, wastepaper basket, which had remained unnoticed until it suddenly burst into flame. I remember a sudden scuffle at the top of the stairs, and then Henry charging down them like a Marathon runner with an oversize torch, and throwing the flaming basket into the Bliss Court passage. There the passage draught fanned it into even fiercer flame until only ashes remained. The heat caused huge blisters and scorching on the passage walls as evidence of Henry's prompt action, and the scars remained until the rebuilding in 1937.'

The contacts that Schollick had made with booksellers far and wide in his first six years with B & M had made him well acquainted with all the problems of the trade, and he proved an admirable and most effective member of the Council of the Booksellers' Association. As we have seen, he was responsible for the very successful development of the Book Tokens scheme. At Oxford he was a tower of strength to Basil and was eventually to become a vice-president of the Company.

HENRY SCHOLLICK

XIII

Gaffer and Staff: 1924–1939

THE main object of the new buildings was, of course, to make room for more stock. Booksellers were being swamped by the flood of new books pouring from the publishers, and the stock in Broad Street had doubled in twenty years. 'Last year', wrote a correspondent in the *Cape Times* in 1934, 'there were 14,608 books published in Britain. . . . One big bookseller, at any rate, seems to solve the difficulty by stocking the lot. . . . But then Blackwell, of course, is more like a public library than a bookseller. He not only stocks practically every book under the sun, but allows you to come in any time and read.' More room was needed, too, for the staff, to say nothing of customers, for the number of people working in the shop and behind the scenes had also doubled since 1919. Three men who were to play an outstanding part in the business had joined the staff during the last few years of Benjamin Henry's life: Will King, Ewart Hine, and Fred Stevens.

In the second decade of this century, my father sat upon the Committee of the City Library which his father had helped to inaugurate. At one of the meetings there was read a letter written with sly humour offering for the acceptance of the Library a considerable collection of standard works in the field of English Literature 'in case frequenters of the Library should still have an itch to read something after exhausting the popular papers on which apparently the Library grant is mainly expended'. The signature was W. King.

My father scrutinized the books and found them to be a poor man's library judiciously chosen, well used, and well kept—the result of many precious sixpences hardly come by. He sought the donor and found him to be a baker's son who had fallen out of employment by the GPO through long illness, and was recovering from a period of almost desperate poverty. In conversation he revealed a mind so stored with reading, so acute in literary judgement, altogether so manifestly the mind of a born bookman, that my father invited him to come and work in the Second-hand and Antiquarian Department of the bookshop. There his knowledge had scope and his personality impressed itself on all who dealt with him, staff and customers alike. Touch his mind at any point and he responded instantly with literary allusions, shrewd criticism, apt folk-sayings, or original aphorisms vividly phrased and presented with the somewhat wry humour of his native Gloucestershire.[1]

'Rex' King was 30 and already a ripe man of letters when he came to Broad Street in 1916, and he served there thirty-four years—*only* thirty-four seems the appropriate qualification for a Blackwellian—until his untimely death in 1950. There he met, and was consulted by, collectors and scholars from Oxford and, indeed, all over the world. One of these, Canon Claude Jenkins of Christ Church, Regius Professor of Ecclesiastical History, had once taught Basil at Magdalen College School, and was a great crony of King's. He was a man of amiable eccentricity, a lover of cats as well as books. He had a habit, at High Table, of secreting toast in the recesses of his gown, for the benefit, it was believed, of his cat family, and bets would be laid on how many pieces he could be observed to gather in during the course of dinner.

He would spend happy hours talking books with Will King, contriving previews of libraries which Will King had bought, a precise punctual man, who surprised King on one occasion by failing to present himself at our old-book warehouse in Alfred Street at 10 o'clock in the morning. King waited for him till nearly a quarter past ten, then locked the door and walked slowly up Alfred Street, but before he reached the High there was a shuffle, and a voice short of breath apologizing for being late: "My housekeeper has just died. Now let us look at the books."[1]

But when he died in 1959, it was found that he had left the first choice of the books in his very large library to a women's college, St. Anne's.

King's visitors would talk to him about literature as well as quartos and octavos. 'Had a satirical encounter with Mr Robert

[1] Basil Blackwell.

Bridges, the Poet Laureate, in the shop this afternoon. Thought how I might have floored him conclusively—30 seconds after his departure.' Thus he wrote in the Journals that he kept intermittently between 1918 and 1939 and bequeathed to Gaffer. For the most part these record his meditations on men and life and God, and the books he read. His reading was very deep and wide. He suffered all his life from ill health, but this literary digestion hardly ever failed him. 'My convalescence was brightened by the perusal of Ferrier's *Institutes of Metaphysics.*' But there were limits even to his appetite. 'Have had a very hard and laborious week at the shop. We have just issued a catalogue of secondhand classical books and there has been a steadily growing stream of orders. As I have tramped from "Ultima Thule" to "Bluebeard's Chamber" or to the Foreign Theological Room, carrying huge folios, or piles of vellum-jacketed quartos, containing the voluminous writings of the early Church Fathers—S. Chrysostom, S. Augustine, S. Ambrose and the rest—I have sung inwardly with great gusto "For all the saints who from their labours rest" and only wished that the more industrious of them had taken their rest a little sooner.'

Hugo Dyson, Fellow and Tutor in English of Basil's college, Merton, and one of King's many friends, read his Journals with deep admiration. 'Rex did not live in a world where the young are paid and begged to read and think and talk and study, but in a world in which you had to pay for and earn all your privileges. If some paid in false coin Rex was not one. For him the whole working world was a great university; he was lucky to find himself in one of the better colleges—the one called Blackwell's.'

Ewart ('Edgar') Hine had served his apprenticeship with H. G. Gadney in Turl Street, and one year as an improver, at 15s. a week, when he was called up in 1917. 'On completing my military service in December 1919', he wrote, 'I was unemployed for two or three weeks, as Mr Gadney had filled my position. It was then, in mid January 1920, that I had a visit from Mr Hunt, the result of which proved to be one of several turning points in my career. Blackwell's were in need of another assistant, and if I was suitable, I would be

invited to join the firm. My first ordeal, as I then thought, on being
offered a post, was the interview with Benjamin Henry Blackwell,
the founder of the firm. To a comparative youngster with not too
much experience, the prospect was a trifle frightening. As I remember, the interview was a pleasant one, with some bargaining
over my starting salary. B.H.B.'s offer was 30s. per week, I pressed
for £2, finally reaching a compromise of 35s. on a month's trial;
that month's trial continued until July 1964 (when he retired) . . .
I was engaged originally as a member of the shop staff, but in those
early years help was given wherever it was needed, and consisted
of writing reports under Harold Cook, help with the Inland Charging
(much of it done by hand then), and trotting round the "Trade".
A job I often did, but did not appreciate, was to place in strict
alphabetical order a long double line of Greek and Latin Classics
with, of course, the help of our Classical Catalogue.' Hine remembered with relish 'Mr Hanks's jubilee celebration at Osse Field in the
1930s when I suppose the staff still only numbered between 60 and 70,
and all those lashings of strawberries and cream'.

Hine is the figure behind the serving desk in the pastel drawing
Muirhead Bone made in 1950. It hung in the Academy that year,
and now hangs in the shop. The Gaffer has written a key to it. (See
overleaf).

Edgar Hine personified 'Blackwell's' for generations of customers
'His calm demeanour, courtesy, and competence won the admiration and confidence of countless visitors. First impressions are of
cardinal importance in book service, and timid freshmen soon learnt
to regard Blackwell's as a friendly and generous institution, for
Edgar's example informed the spirit of the serving staff.'[1] He met,
and often made friends of, many eminent men in the course of his
long service.

I still have clear memories [he wrote in 1964] of Mr Asquith, living in
retirement at Sutton Courtenay, Robert Bridges, the then Poet Laureate,
at Boars Hill, the first Lord Birkenhead, and two very great gentlemen,
John Buchan and John Masefield. I remember, too, an early meeting I
had with Walter de la Mare, who we had previously been warned

[1] Basil Blackwell.

BLACKWELL'S, OXFORD, 1950

A pastel drawing by Muirhead Bone. (*For key see facing page*)

would be in Oxford on a certain day. A copy or two of his book of poems 'Peacock Pie' were placed in the window and he, having noticed them, was curious to know who had been responsible. I was then introduced to him and he was gracious enough to buy and autograph a copy for me. During the war, J. B. Priestley and W. B. Yeats made their homes in Oxford. Distinguished literary men of a much later generation included W. H. Auden, Stephen Spender, C. Day Lewis, and John Betjeman.

In 1952, Hine and Stevens were elected to the Board, 'a promotion we did not expect or one which we thought deserved. From office boy to director—something beyond my wildest dreams.'

Fred Stevens also joined Blackwell's in 1920, a few months after Hine. He had been in the army for three years and then worked with the War Pensions Committee. He was one of the backroom boys in Broad Street, and helped to lay the foundations of the firm's enormous Periodicals Department, which now accounts for over half of the total sales.

He was introduced to us by his fiancée Maggie Warner, the third in line of my father's secretaries. The first (the first young woman to work at Blackwell's) had proved too upsetting for the male staff and had made

---

The Gaffer's key to Muirhead Bone's drawing on facing page.

On the right is the Revd. Colin Stephenson, Vicar of St. Mary Magdalen and later Chaplain of the Slipper Chapel at Walsingham. Beyond him Colin Roberts, Secretary to the Delegates,[1] J. D. Mabbott, President of St. John's, and the fine figure in the centre of Professor Hugh Last, Principal of Brasenose. (G. N. Clark originally posed for this position, but was dismissed by Bone as not being of sufficient height and dignity, and Last was sent for). Seated on the left is an undergraduate . . . D. L. Edwards of Magdalen.[2] Behind him is Professor Garrod, my Mods tutor, of Merton, and in the far distance Enid Starkie (in all the colours of the Rimbaud!— a witticism attributed to me but above my blood. I tackled Bowra on this head, but he denied it). At the foot of the staircase, seen in profile, is son Richard; coming down the staircase—myself.

[1] Of the Clarendon Press, 1954–75.   [2] Now Dean of Norwich.

way for a discreet red-haired maiden who lived in the odour of sanctity; she married, and Maggie was doubly to be thanked, for her own services and for this propitious introduction.[1]

Stevens, too, has left some reminiscences of his time in Broad Street.

My main task was to deal with the orders for periodicals, which were regarded as a nuisance by the booksellers. At that time the turnover was small, perhaps about £2,000 per annum, but I found a few large orders from overseas libraries who had asked Blackwell's to look after their subscriptions for periodicals and, if possible, to fill the gaps in their sets caused by the first World War. From then on new library orders came in gradually, by recommendation from one librarian to another. . . . In 1933, we produced our first Catalogue of Periodicals.

Then came the Second World War and we were cut off from most of our overseas suppliers and many of our customers. This was the only time in the history of the Periodicals Department when the sales dropped, and I, together with some other men from the shop, was glad to work 24 hours a week with the Royal Observer Corps. The period 1945–68 was a time of considerable expansion and by the year 1968 when I retired the sales had almost reached two million pounds per annum. In other words, we had nearly added three noughts to the 1920 figure.[2]

He had then been a director for sixteen years, and could look back with pride on a truly remarkable record. 'Fred Stevens', said Richard Blackwell, 'was the embodiment of all the Blackwell virtues, dedication to hard work, customer service, and "acc'racy", and a deep-seated conviction that any labour-saving device or method indicated lack of moral fibre.'

In 1925 George Bunting joined the company as a post-boy at 15s. a week, to retire 52 years later as a director, and to remain linked to the firm as a vice-president. It was on 1 January 1927 that he was instructed to report to Will Hunt in the Order Department 'to learn the art of mail order bookselling'. Some measure of the extent of this art at that time may be seen in the fact that all mail order was dealt with in a tiny room, no more than ten feet square,

---

[1] Basil Blackwell.

[2] The further expansion of the periodicals department is described in Chapter XVII.

which many visitors to the shop premises will remember as the Counting House on the first mezzanine floor. Will Hunt occupied a large oak desk, which Benjamin Henry Blackwell had bought in 1884 at the auction of Charles Reade's furniture after his death. The desk was returned to Magdalen College 50 years later by Basil Blackwell, in commemoration of the author, with the addition of a small engraved plate which read

> I, when Charles Reade had breathed his last,
> For Hard Cash to a bookshop passed;
> Now, as a gift returned, I claim
> The Hearth and Cloister whence I came.

The only other desk in the cramped office was shared—though only one person at a time could be seated—by Bunting and Percy Coates, who had been apprenticed in 1919. Bunting's long experience of mail-order bookselling was to bear fruit after the war when this side of the business expanded so vastly and so fast.

The old order of things, under which most recruits to the business arrived as young boys straight from their elementary schools to serve their apprenticeship, was beginning to pass away after the 1914–18 war, and when Basil succeeded his father he started to recruit boys—and girls—from the local secondary schools. It was thus that the girl who was to become his peerless secretary for nearly forty years came to Broad Street. 'Miss Halliday was the most incredibly efficient person I have ever known. She was also the greatest darling. For years I have regarded her as one of my dearest friends, but we never met. I knew her only on the telephone, always helpful, always kind, always right. Her voice delighted me; it was the very breath of goodness and gaiety. How odd to be brought to the verge of tears by the death of a woman one has never seen.' So wrote Edmond Segrave, editor of the *Bookseller*, about Basil's secretary, Eleanor (Mrs Atkinson at home, but at work she remained Miss Eleanor Halliday), who died prematurely of lung cancer in 1968. She had come from Milham Ford School in 1928 with the strong recommendation of an admirable headmistress, Miss McCabe, and a few School Certificates to her credit. Technical qualifications were not

ELEANOR AND THE GAFFER, 1950

thought necessary in those days. It was quite normal to leave school at about 16 and learn your job by doing it. After two years' work in the Foreign Department under Jan Bijl (later to become a bookseller on his own account) had revealed her quality, Basil had her instructed in shorthand and typing, and she became his secretary. 'She gave me the whole loyalty of her generous spirit and devoted her boundless energy to the service of the firm in all its aspects. She never betrayed a confidence, and won the confidence of all; she never reckoned the hours—she would work the whole day through and more also without rest—nothing, not even the emotional stresses of preparing for marriage, impaired the thorough quality of her work. She had no moods, she never quarrelled; work was an honest task to be done and offered no reasonable ground for disagreement. She knew all the procedure of bookselling and publishing, and could help out any section in difficulties.' When she died the Gaffer felt she had taken with her 'half my competence'. Her memory is preserved by a bequest to the library of Magdalen College School.[1]

As the reader will have gathered by now, the Gaffer was a firm believer in paternalism, and this did not just mean concern and affection for this family of his. It had its very practical side. He wanted each and every one of them to take a personal interest in the success and well-being of the firm. In addition to the formal and stated Board Meetings, the directors met informally, almost every week, in the Chairman's office. The records of these lively meetings, carefully preserved and labelled 'Personal Property of Mr Basil', show that their knowledge of everything that was going on in Broad Street was, like Mr Weller's knowledge of London, 'extensive and peculiar'. They discussed everything, from current sales figures, wages, and reluctant debtors to 'dusting and weeding' and impending marriages. Suggestions were made and decisions taken. The Chairman, for example, 'undertook to experiment as to the dryness of the cellar by storing there a quantity of the *Modern Churchman* and *Blackfriars*, results to be carefully watched' (20 January 1933). There was another, somewhat less high-powered, group called the Archimandrites—heads of departments mostly—which met from time

[1] Basil Blackwell.

to time, and to whose collective wisdom and valuable suggestions the Chairman often referred at Board Meetings. It was 'open management' at its best.

Meanwhile a future chairman was growing up. In 1931 Basil's elder son, Richard, won a scholarship to Winchester from the Dragon School, and wrote to thank Critchley for the letter of congratulation sent to him by the Directors. 'Almost as soon as I entered College I learnt that "Blackwell's" is well known to my form master, who has pointed me out as "the grandson". I shall try to live up to the reputation Blackwell's has here.' He became an oarsman like his father, and was President of the school boat club in his last year, and he won a scholarship to New College. By 1939,

Corinna Penelope B.B. Richard
Christine Julian Helen

THE FAMILY, 1935

when the firm celebrated its sixtieth birthday, and Richard his twenty-first, he had been allotted 50 shares in B. H. Blackwell Ltd. and was beginning to read Greats (after a First in Mods), but the war, in which he served in the Royal Navy, cut short his university career and postponed his initiation into the mysteries of the book trade.

XIV

The Second World War

THE British who went to war in 1939 were no less valiant than their fathers twenty-five years earlier, nor less stubborn, but, as a nation, they were better educated, and more aware. They could not, perhaps, have put up so long with the stagnant carnage of trench warfare, but, because they had fewer illusions, they may have been the better able to face without dismay the military disasters of 1940 and 1941. The growth that had taken place in secondary and university education certainly helped them to resist, and finally overcome, all the 'crafts and assaults' of their enemies. Without that growth there would have been, in 1939, a much smaller number of young people able to tackle the complications of the modern war machine. It was soon found that a young man whose education had stopped short at the elementary stage could not be trained quickly, or easily, to fly a Spitfire or navigate a bomber. The Battle of Britain, it may almost be said, was won, not on the playing fields of Eton, but in the classrooms of the new grammar schools.

In the earlier war booksellers had had a bad time. Blackwell's sales had fallen by a third, and in 1939 the directors agreed that history must be expected to repeat itself. There was, indeed, a drop of about 12 per cent in the first year, but at the end of the second the Chairman found himself commenting on the growing demand for books throughout the country, 'a demand which is outstripping supplies and must lead presently to a book famine'. The 'New Reading Public' that had been the theme of Basil's Ripon Hall conference in 1934 wanted more books than ever. In December 1940 sales were a record for the month, and by the end of the war annual sales were running at more than double the 1939 level.

Those in the book trade, like everyone else, had to endure many tribulations and many inconveniences, but in one respect they had 'never had it so good'. They found that they could sell everything they produced and sell it quickly. The trouble was that they could not produce enough. The labour force of printers and binders was depleted by the needs of war, and paper was severely rationed. During most of the war a publisher was allowed only 40 per cent of his pre-war consumption, though the use of thinner paper, smaller type, and narrower margins made the ration go further. The shortage of labour bore most hard on the output of new books, which fell by more than a half during the war. Reprints involved no work in the composing rooms, and came off better. In general, more copies of fewer books were produced. Fine printing was, of course, out of the question, and the Shakespeare Head Press could no longer perform its prime function, but it was entitled to its quota of paper, like any other publishing business. Henry Schollick saw to it that this quota was fully used, to produce austerity books instead of luxuries.

Restricted supply and insatiable demand did in time lead to the book famine foretold by Blackwell in 1941. Publishers began to ration their customers, and old-timers in Broad Street recalled the days when, if you wanted fifty copies of a book, you ordered a hundred and hoped for the best. Second-hand copies of some essential books fetched fancy prices. A copy of the *Concise Oxford Dictionary* was advertised one day in a London newspaper at £4, though its published price—if you could find a new copy—was still only 10s. 6d.

The publishers might have had their supplies of paper even more severely rationed if they had not been able to show what a large proportion of their books was exported. To produce overall figures for a trade which, as R. J. L. Kingsford remarks in his history of *The Publishers Association, 1896–1946*, 'had constantly rejected any peace-time demand for statistics as an unjustifiable inquisition', was a notable achievement by the Association. The result surprised even the publishers, still more the Board of Trade. Some of the larger publishers were found to be exporting 50 per cent or more, and the average turned out to be about one-third. These figures, high as they were, took no account of exports by the retailers. The importance of maintaining book exports, and not for solely economic reasons, was in everyone's mind, and in the late summer of 1940 Blackwell's sent out a printed circular 'as from a British Bookseller' to friends in America.

Many of you feel that there is nothing that you personally can do to help us here and now. But there *is* one thing that any friend overseas can do, at once and easily, and that is to buy a book produced in this Homeland of ours and encourage your friends to do likewise. All the ideals we are fighting for are enshrined in our books, even our novels describe the way of ordinary social life which is now threatened. You share our ideals, and the best of our culture has a common source. The future of the free peoples is full of hope if they understand one another and work open-eyed together. Everything that contributes to that end is helping to win, and end, this war. Meantime, every coin you spend on a British book helps us to fight more effectively. . . . Do not think you can do nothing if you cannot make big purchases; *buy just one book*. We can choose for you one or two of the books which are characteristically British, or which are specially interesting people over here today. . . . Money spent on strengthening those ties between us, which are vital to us all, will do something at once to fight down the threats of tyranny.

There were no air raids on Oxford throughout the war and no 'doodlebugs' or V2s fell on the city, but the Air Raid Precautions services had to be kept in a high state of readiness. The staff in Broad Street played their part as Wardens, Fire Watchers, and Observers, and two members slept on the premises every night. But George's were in the thick of it in Bristol, which was frequently and heavily attacked. George's were lucky to escape with only superficial damage, but neighbouring booksellers had their premises and stock completely destroyed, and were invited to operate temporarily from George's shop. Some, however, never recovered from the effects of enemy action. There were fewer shops to serve a public greatly enlarged by evacuation from London and elsewhere, and George's prospered exceedingly. Turnover had increased by more than 20 per cent by 1945, but the wartime Excess Profits Tax ensured that the increase in profits went to the Exchequer.

The destruction in Bristol and other towns was nothing to what took place in London on the night of 29–30 December 1940. In a concentrated attack on the City by high-explosive and incendiary bombs the Germans succeeded in laying waste the historic centre of the British book trade in and around Paternoster Row. Several large publishers—Longman, Nelson, Hutchinson, Collins among them—lost their premises and more than a million books. Worse still, the great wholesale firm of Simpkin Marshall, a vital link in the trade between publisher and bookseller, was totally destroyed. Bulk supplies of new books had always gone, of course, direct from the publishers to the bookshops, but the retailers sent their daily orders for single copies and small 'repeats' to Simpkin's, who held a very large reservoir of stock from all the publishers 'on consignment'. The use of a single channel for the supply of thousands of different titles to hundreds of shops from scores of publishers was a great boon to the trade, and its loss a grievous blow. Efforts to revive the system after the war came to nothing.

The war proved how little harm most of us take from having to work harder than usual, if our hearts are in it. Blackwell's (and George's) were, like other booksellers, very short-handed. At the twenty-fifth Annual General Meeting in December 1944 the Chairman recorded that there were 30 of his men and 18 women serving in the Forces—21 of the men overseas. The work for those left behind, helped though they were by a temporary intake of teenagers, was made the heavier by many necessary but time-consuming wartime regulations and restrictions. But there was, no doubt, satisfaction in knowing that somehow the work got done and that the business prospered (the jubilee AGM was appropriately celebrated by declaring a dividend of 25 per cent—for the first time), and the family feeling was kept warm by the Gaffer by 'periodical encyclicals' to the absent members, to give them news from the home front in Broad Street. Not the least welcome news, conveyed from time to time, was that the firm was paying up their pension contributions. Fortunately only one of them lost his life: a young man, Burborough, who had come as an apprentice, and who was killed in Burma. George's also lost one man, Butlin, who may well have been the first war casualty in the book trade. He was in the merchantman *Yorkshire* when she was sunk by a German submarine, and was last seen giving up his place in a lifeboat to two women.

A new publishing venture by the Gaffer, arising out of the Nuffield endowment of medical research at Oxford in 1936, and already mentioned briefly at the end of Chapter IX, began to bear fruit during the war. The future Lord Nuffield (W. R. Morris was created Baronet in 1929 and Viscount in 1938) began his long and carefully planned series of benefactions to medicine in 1927. At first it was the care and cure of the sick that benefited. By 1934 he had given over £500,000 to hospitals in Birmingham, London and, of course, Oxford, and this was only the beginning. But he wished also to do something for medical education and research. The undergraduates who got their preclinical education in the Honours School of Physiology at Oxford went on to the teaching hospitals in London and elsewhere to complete their training. Could not a postgraduate school of medical research be established in Oxford with the Radcliffe Infirmary and the University working in partnership? The great idea was discussed and worked out in consultations with the Regius Professor of Medicine, Sir Farquhar Buzzard, and the Registrar of the University, Douglas Veale. In 1936 the plans were ready and in a letter to the Vice-Chancellor Morris offered the University £1¼ million to endow a Medical School Trust. When the proposal to accept this magnificent benefaction came before a special meeting of Congregation presided over by the Chancellor, Lord Halifax, up rose Sir William Morris and sought permission to amend the sum to £2 million, as he had heard in the meantime that the larger sum would be needed to do the thing properly. The amendment was carried.

The Gaffer soon saw the implications of a benefaction that was sure to transform, and has transformed, the Oxford Medical School and the Oxford hospitals. He began to confer with Buzzard, and at the directors' meeting in January 1938 he said that 'the Company might be very well advised to consider the development of a medical publishing and bookselling side in conjunction with Blackwell and Mott'. An energetic young Scot, John Grant, who had had a spell of training in Broad Street before going into the family firm of Oliver and Boyd in Edinburgh, had soon decided that he preferred Broad Street, and had recently joined the staff. It was he who first suggested the new enterprise and he was instructed to prepare a memorandum on the prospects. In February 1939 a new company, Blackwell Scientific Publications Ltd., was formed, with Grant as managing director. It was to be responsible 'for the publication and sale of medical and scientific research books, the formation of a medical lending library, and, if possible, the publication of a Nuffield Journal'. Thus, on the eve of war, was founded a subsidiary that was to grow into one of the most successful of all Blackwell enterprises. 'BSP's first book, *The Essentials of Anaesthesia* by Professor R. R. Macintosh, appeared in November 1940 and quickly sold out. By 1942 the second printing was half sold and two more titles were in preparation. 'This young firm has made a very good start' said the Chairman at the Annual General Meeting in December 1942. Its avowed policy was to publish only 'pioneer books of the very first order', and it was already paying dividends. It was not many years before BSP became one of the foremost medical publishing houses in Britain.[1]

Meanwhile the parent firm of Blackwell and Mott, seventeen years old in 1939, fared much the same during the war as other publishers, especially those involved in the educational field: badly at first, perplexingly well thereafter. The London County Council, a very important customer, ceased to buy books when war broke out (their schools had all been evacuated), there was, at first, no compensating increase in sales elsewhere, and turnover fell by a third. The future, in September 1940, looked so gloomy that it did not seem a great disaster to the Directors when, on the 27th, German bombs destroyed all their unbound stocks of school and children's books held by Billings, the Guildford printers. The loss was, to be sure, partly covered by the (compulsory) War Risks Insurance scheme, and they congratulated themselves, moreover, on being

[1] See Chapter XX.

able to offset some of the rest by selling the sheets of slow-selling books, warehoused elsewhere, at 2*d*. a pound for wrapping purposes! It seemed a sensible decision in that dark autumn, but they lived to regret it. They were not the only publishers to read the omens wrong. The Oxford University Press, for example, well provided as they were with slow sellers, happily pulped 'surplus' stocks of many books that would have sold fast in the future. They even proposed to reduce their enormous unbound stock of the Oxford English Dictionary, but an Air Raid Warden demonstrated that the tons of sheets, formed into a hollow square, made an exceptionally secure Wardens' Post in the Jordan Hill warehouse in North Oxford, and the Dictionary was reprieved.

The upturn in sales took place very quickly. In the second year of the war B & M's shot up by nearly £4,000 and, like other publishers, they began to ration their customers, for the shortages of paper and labour, as we have seen, made it impossible to keep pace with the demand. Profits soared, too, from under £500 a year before the war to nearly £9,000 by the end of it, only to be swallowed up by the Inland Revenue by way of Excess Profits Tax. Even so, there was a liquidity problem, for though the tax restricted the Company's real growth, receipts from sales could not be used fast enough to replenish the shrinking reservoir of stock, and some of the unemployable cash had to be stowed away in War Loan and the like. For the Annual General Meeting in December 1945 Basil asked Henry Schollick to make a report on the last war year, and this reflects very clearly the course of wartime publication. In 1939 the Company had consumed 53 tons of paper. In 1945 their ration was 23 tons, though Henry's 'careful husbandry' had added 14 more by special licences for 'essential books' and other subtle but lawful means. They had produced 51 books, 20 new and 31 reprints, but only in the face of great difficulties in finding printers and binders to manufacture them. Barfoot and Fenemore had worked like Trojans with a depleted and largely inexperienced staff to cope with a turnover nearly twice as large as before the war. But the future had not been lost sight of. After the fall of France in 1940 it had, of course, become impossible to import French (or German) texts for school and university use, and a new series, initiated by Blackwell and Mott, and edited by the two Oxford Professors, had now established itself. It gave the firm, as Uncle Henry remarked with satisfaction, 'an entry into the select preserves of the set books formerly produced by the University Presses'. It was to bear useful fruit in the years to come.

RICHARD BLACKWELL

XV

After the War: Booksellers to the World

IN 1946 the third generation joined the family firm. Richard Blackwell, the Gaffer's elder son, came home from the war, during which he had spent more than six years in the Navy, on convoy duty in northern waters, and in the Mediterranean, and had been awarded the DSC. He was 28. He joined a firm with an annual turnover of £165,000. Thirty-three years later, in Blackwell's centenary year, the turnover was more than £27 million. That was the measure of Richard's achievement. He would assert, in his deprecating way, that it had just been a matter of taking advantage of promising conditions. 'Others went to sleep. We didn't. No need to make a long story of it.' Not so long, maybe, as can properly be made of events further back in time, more firmly lodged in history, but not too short a story either. If the earlier part of this history might well be called 'The Book of the Gaffer' the later part equally deserves to be called 'The Book of the Guv'nor' for as such he was known.

The longest-serving and most impressive of the Gaffer's colleagues, Fred Hanks, still a hale and hearty man in his eighties who had come to Broad Street in 1883, extended an avuncular welcome to the Founder's grandson. He wrote in the company's recently inaugurated house journal, the *Broad Sheet*, 'As the heir to a goodly heritage, we all wish him Godspeed in maintaining the sound traditions of the business instituted by his grandfather, and so pleasantly developed by his father. Floreat!' Richard's reply took note of his responsibilities. 'I am duly sensible of my good fortune in coming into a business, the name of which stands so high all over the world, and in joining the staff who are responsible for this reputation. . . . I am most grateful for all the help and wisdom given to me and for all that I feel sure will be given.'

Basil expected to see his son succeed him as head of the firm, and determined that he should have freedom to develop his own ideas. The future would be his, and he should play a main part in shaping it. So Richard was given a roving commission to familiarize himself with every part of the firm's operations. He watched and he questioned, and, three years later, in June 1949, in a paper entitled 'Specialization', he put before the Chairman and Directors his proposals for reorganization. 'Now that the firm has grown to this size, it is perhaps a good thing to ask ourselves whether our organization is best suited to our needs.'

Three factors in the outlook for the book trade forcibly impressed him: the importance of exports, the part played by mail-order sales, and the signs of a worldwide expansion in education. Richard's target was growth, on a scale hardly as yet contemplated, and for which Blackwell's was not yet well enough prepared, though even he can hardly have envisaged growth so rapid and huge as was to be achieved in the next thirty years.

To export was a matter of national expediency as well as private advantage, and British books were already doing well in this field. The bulk of the trade was of course in the hands of the producers, the publishers, but a few booksellers had built up a considerable business in direct sales to customers overseas. Blackwell's, as we have seen, were pre-eminent in the Indian market, and had made some valuable contacts elsewhere. The Indian trade, however, had been upset by the war, and was still further reduced by the effects of Independence and Partition in 1948. But this loss would be more than made good. In September 1949 the pound was devalued against the dollar by 30 per cent and British books, along with other commodities, became that much cheaper, and more marketable, in the USA.

Mail-order sales were no new thing in Broad Street. The Founder had long ago, in some of his early catalogues, drawn attention to the advantages of low postal rates. By 1939 the Company's mailing

RICHARD BLACKWELL

list contained over 20,000 addresses, of which more than a third related to customers abroad, and all these must have been buying by mail order. The same was doubtless true of most of the UK customers living outside Oxford. But the bulk of such business was not in fact very great. In 1946 the export department still consisted of only six people, and was housed in a corner of the basement of Trinity College library. One man could usually carry by himself, in one load, all the incoming stock needed for a day's orders. Richard Blackwell returned from a tour of bookselling businesses in the north of England in 1948 to report that 'all the forward bookshops are concentrating on the selling of books by mail order; and we cannot afford *not* to be in the forefront here'.

The postwar expansion in education was well under way in 1949, at home and abroad. More and more students were pouring into the universities, and it was evident that new universities would have to be established to cater for hugely increased numbers. Each new university would need a library and the library would need a full range of standard university textbooks and reference books, and as quickly as possible. Here was a promising field indeed for the academic bookseller, and Richard meant his firm to compete in it vigorously. But he was in no doubt that its methods would have to be changed. Reorganization was indeed overdue, for the firm had already grown too big for the old methods to produce the best results. Richard's proposed solution was what he called 'specialization'.

It was not something entirely new, something unheard of, that he was proposing. Not long after the Founder had set up in business he had found it desirable to classify his stock into separate subject sections, and give one assistant the chief responsibility for each. Second-hand books were a class distinct from all others and had for many years had specialist treatment. A separate periodicals department had been set up soon after the 1914–18 war. But apart from these two cases specialization was not rigid. There was a general feeling that everyone ought to know something about everything. This, in Richard's view, was no longer the right idea. Too many books were pouring out from the publishers for anyone to be a successful all-round expert—and it was expert service, in every branch of knowledge, that was required to cater for the needs of the new generation of university librarians rapidly growing up abroad. Scholarship was becoming international, and English its *lingua franca*. From its origins as a small university bookshop Blackwell's had grown into one of the largest national bookshops in Britain. They now had an opportunity, if they made the right preparation for it, to become booksellers to the world.

It was natural that Richard's proposals should be viewed critically by the more senior members of the staff. There were twenty-seven of them who had been Blackwellians for more than sixteen years— some a good deal more—and their doubts arose from their loyalty to the firm and their belief in the wisdom of its time-honoured methods. But they came to recognize the necessity, if not the desirability, of change. 'The scholar-bookseller', wrote Will King to the Gaffer in 1950, 'is an anachronism in this giddy age. . . . It was only in Victorian days that a bookseller like the one depicted in Beatrice Harraden's novel *Ships that Pass in the Night* could ejaculate that so long as he had a shelf full of Gibbon and a box full of snuff he was quite content.' Richard's arguments won the day in the end and the new order was established.

Commercial courtesy and prudence dictate that 'the customer is always right'. The rule of the Guv'nor reinforced this common-sensical approach and, tempered by the realities of the practical and economic, elevated it to the dogmatic inspiration of his enterprise.

XVI

Specialists in Action

Two of the notable achievements in specialization at Blackwell's have been in two of the oldest subjects in the academic field, Theology and Classics. New men were brought in, soon after Richard's 'manifesto', to take charge of these ancient provinces, and given a free hand to cultivate them intensively. Christopher Francis came to take charge of theology in 1952. He had already acquired a wide knowledge of the subject during years spent in searching for a vocation to enter the religious life, a vocation that he decided that he had failed to find, and he had also some experience of bookselling. Theology had long fallen behind in importance in the shop, and the department was rather a backwater. The new manager decided to start by compiling a new catalogue to replace the existing Annual General Catalogue, in which theology occupied only eighteen pages. He saw the need for a comprehensive bibliography of the available literature, English and foreign, and devised a new system of classification to cover the whole field. When completed the theology section of the new catalogue ran to 108 pages, out of all proportion to the size and status of his department. To those who were still opposed to 'specialization' this seemed absurd, but Richard gave it his full support. The catalogue was duly printed and despatched—and the response exceeded all expectations. Orders came pouring in, and with them many letters of appreciation.

It proved to be a remarkable vindication of specialization. Francis himself wrote, many years later: 'It is true that in the fifties and sixties our Theology Department seemed to be supplying the whole world and to be unique in its stock and its service, but I am anxious to give the credit for this where it rightly belongs. In the first place it was due to Mr Richard Blackwell. . . . This idea of specialization was his and without his unfailing support and the resources he put at our disposal we could have done nothing.' True, but it was Chris Francis's special gifts and energies that made Blackwell's Theology Department so famous. He was much more than an efficient supplier of current books. His encyclopaedic knowledge of the subject was known to, and willingly made available to, theologians all over the world, and a visit to Blackwell's came to be an essential item on the agenda of every visiting scholar to Oxford.

Francis crowned his work by producing, in 1978,[1] a comprehensive *Catalogue of Theology and Church History* running to 246 pages (no. 1120 in the Blackwell series), 'an important work of scholarship and bibliography in its own right', as it was described by Professor James O'Donnell of Cornell University. It contains a discerning and affectionate tribute from Francis's old friend Henry Chadwick, formerly Regius Professor of Divinity at Oxford, latterly Dean of Christ Church, and now Regius Professor at Cambridge: 'For two decades, Christopher Francis has been integral not only to one of the greatest of academic bookshops, but also to the serious study of religion and theology in the English-speaking world.'

Classics had long been a subject of prime importance for the academic bookseller. Apprentices at Blackwell's were handed a pamphlet prepared for their education by Fred Hanks entitled 'On the Handling of Classical Books'. So far so good, but here, too, it was decided to try the effects of expert and intensive specialization. Paul Quinton was enlisted from London University in 1951, and by means of new and more comprehensive catalogues mailed to a constantly growing list of customers, the Classics Department, like the Theology Department, achieved an international reputation. The first Prime Minister of Israel, David Ben Gurion, a keen Platonist, was a regular visitor. One such visit attracted the notice of the *New Statesman*: 'In an age of barbarism it is a pleasant thought that anyone who penetrated to the back rooms of Blackwell's last week

[1] In May 1980 the university conferred on him the degree of MA *honoris causa*. On his retirement from the Board of Blackwell's he was made a vice-president of the Company.

and spied a little white-haired man on the top of the step ladder would have seen a Prime Minister indulging his secret vice.'

Music was a different matter. Though the Heather Professorship of Music founded in 1627 is one of the oldest Chairs in Oxford, a full faculty of music was not instituted till 1944, and the academic study of music was a comparative rarity till then. There were practical marketing problems, too. Customers would be best served if they could buy not only books on music, but music too, and, for that matter, records. But music, especially sheet music, and records would be difficult to handle in Broad Street. So the setting up of a separate music department had been postponed, though the great popularity of the subject certainly justified it. By a happy chance the Gaffer discovered, early in the fifties, that Frederick Dymond, a man with a wide knowledge of music and twenty years experience of bookselling at Heffer's of Cambridge, was available. He was engaged and put in charge of a newly created department of music. When he retired in 1974 to the strains of a farewell concert given by Norman Del Mar, Manouk Parikian, and other distinguished musical friends, the department had long been housed in a new and specially designed building in Holywell. It is believed to be the largest (and busiest) shop of its kind in Britain, supplying almost everything musical except instruments.

The fourth special department to be noticed in this chapter, Antiquarian Books, did not come into existence as a result of post-war reorganization. Antiquarian books had been the staple part of the Founder's stock-in-trade in 1879, and although in course of time the sale of new books became the principal business of the firm, antiquarian bookselling was never neglected. Will King had been in charge of the department for many years when he died in 1950. He was succeeded by Edward East, who himself had joined the firm, as an apprentice, in 1923, only seven years after King. East maintained, and even enhanced, the prestige and prosperity of the department. In 1973, when he had completed fifty years in the service of Blackwell's, the Gaffer paid tribute to him. 'Your mastery of book-lore is acclaimed by bibliographers and collectors in all parts of the English speaking world, and your integrity has won the confidence

FYFIELD MANOR

Barry Moser 1979

of learned libraries small and great from Bodley to Folger.' In the same year the University conferred the degree of MA on him *honoris causa*. He was succeeded by Peter Fenemore, son of 'Fen' (see Chapter VII).

The further growth of the department was limited by the inadequacy of its cramped quarters in Ship Street, and it was decided to follow the example of a number of Antiquarian businesses and move into the country. Fyfield Manor, a stone house dating from the early fourteenth century, and described by Pevsner as 'a remarkable survival', was bought and converted to the department's use. It was originally the home of the Golafre family, and we are told that Dean Swift resided there for some time and that Lemuel Gulliver derives his name from Golafre. 'Fyfield' was opened in October 1979 and a special Centenary Antiquarian Catalogue was issued to mark the occasion.

A tapestry of the arms of the Golafre family was presented, for rehanging at Fyfield Manor, by Mrs John Garton, who had lived there for many years. The photograph shows Richard Blackwell acknowledging the gift. This was his last ceremony, and he left his hospital bed to attend it.

XVII

The Periodicals Division

IT is a surprising fact that at the end of the firm's first hundred years more than half the annual turnover came from the sale, not of books, but of periodicals. The origins of this branch of business, just after the first war, have been described in chapter XIII. It was initiated not so much for its own sake as to oblige customers valued for their book orders. The first of these was the University of Cape Town, which sent in a substantial order for periodicals in 1919. But the profit margin on them was small. 'Periodicals were regarded as a nuisance by booksellers', as Fred Stevens said. Sales, however, grew steadily, and within twenty years had risen from £3,000 a year to £16,000, and from one-sixteenth of Blackwell's total turnover to well over one-tenth. Periodicals were, after all, proving to be big enough business to be worth cultivating for their own sake.

After the second war the scene changed dramatically. Much research had remained unpublished during the war, a huge amount of new material was being produced by the growing university populations, and new periodicals were being rapidly launched to cater for these increasing demands. By the late fifties Blackwell's sales had reached £250,000, by 1963 £500,000, and in 1968, when Stevens retired, having been a director of the firm for the previous sixteen years, the figure was £2,000,000. Under his successor, John Merriman, who became a director in 1971, sales continued to rise at an astonishing speed (partly boosted by inflation), to £4,000,000 in 1973, £6,500,000 in 1975, over £10,000,000 in 1977, and so to over £17,000,000 by the centenary year.

In 1979 the Periodicals Division, handling subscriptions to journals published throughout the five continents for supply to libraries and institutions in all parts of the world, serviced over 350,000 subscription records. The bizarre variety of subject matter was illustrated by Richard Blackwell in an address to an academic audience some years ago. He cited

The Bulletin of Tibetology, *The Dancing Times*, and *The Delius Society*; a journal in Welsh whose title I could not pronounce, nor you understand; *The Irish Ancestor* and *The Journal of Byelorussian Studies*; *The Japanese Journal of Educational Psychology* and *The Lancashire Dialect Society*; *The Marshall McLuhan Dewline Newsletter*, *Northamptonshire Past and Present* and *The Review of Korean Economy*; *The Shavian* and *The Swansea Geographer*; *Blanco y Negro*, an intermittent weekly published in Madrid, and *Bianco e Nero*, a monthly published in Rome; *The Collection of Czechoslovak Chemical Communications*; *Tetrahedron* and *Nature*, and *Aeronautical Quarterly*; three journals with the title, if translated, *Geodesy and Cartography*, published in Hungary, Poland, and Russia; and the *Zeitschrift für Wahrscheinlichkeitstheorie und verwandte Gebiete*. On the latest list that we have been sent is an order for a subscription to a magazine of the Arts published in Bombay with the title *Damn You*. This reflects our sentiments, as we cannot at the moment discover from where to order it.

Apart from diversity, and sheer numbers—estimates of the number of journals in existence have varied from 30,000 to 70,000, but nobody knows—there are uncertainties peculiar to the lives of periodicals that make trouble for the distributor. A journal may change its editor, its publisher, its subscription rates, even its title. The enormous expansion achieved by the Periodicals Division in the seventies in a field so extensive, and so full of pitfalls, would not have been possible by means till then regarded as normal. It was the concentration of all mail order business in Beaver House in 1973 (mentioned in a later chapter) and the setting up of control by computer that enabled John Merriman to quadruple his turnover in six years.

There are some solid advantages to compensate for the difficulties of handling the sale of journals. Even the private subscriber tends to remain a subscriber for life, and libraries feel a sort of obligation to go on for ever. In hard times they would rather economize in the purchase of books than cut their journal subscriptions. The learned journal has acquired a greater importance in higher education. Far more research is being carried out, and the journal article is the most efficient and rapid way in which its results can be made available. The creation of so many new libraries since the war has also led to an unprecedented demand for back numbers, or their equivalent in microfilm editions. This branch of the business was contributing more than £750,000 to turnover in 1979, and has had its own specialist manager, Charles Wickert, since 1958.

The peculiarities of the Journal Business, which call for subscriptions to be paid in advance for the succeeding year, call for a high order of financial control and acumen, established in the early fifties by Cecil Palmer. When he was translated to the post of Company Secretary *per se* a decade later his former acolyte 'George' Wareham continued to develop the requisite techniques of the appropriate financial husbandry so essential to the service.

XVIII

New Shop Windows in Oxford:
Julian Blackwell takes a Hand

WHEN the new building in Broad Street, on the site of Nos. 48 and 49 and Bliss Court, was completed in 1938, the directors hoped that the extra space would generate enough extra business to justify the outlay. They little thought that, on the contrary, business would grow so fast after the war that they would soon have to hive off some departments into other buildings. The first to move out were children's books. They had by then acquired a sort of departmental status, in a small room for small people. A schoolgirl customer, Elizabeth Taylor, has left a description of it. 'The children's department was deep inside the building, walled in on all sides with a richness of books, with alcoves lined with them and tables heaped with them. . . . I cannot have been the only child in the bookshop, but perhaps I was the most constant reader. In later years, I was told that Basil Blackwell himself would occasionally include me in the sights he pointed out to visitors he showed round his bookshop.' It was a magic cave, but not big enough. In 1950 the Children's Bookshop came into being across the road, at 22 Broad Street, a little old three-storey house with very narrow staircases. Marjorie Genese, who had joined Blackwell's soon after the war to take charge of the department, cheerfully accepted the help of some of her young customers for the move. 'For weeks we carried books about—sorting, arranging, categorising and stacking. There were three floors, each one a challenge to the achievement of maximum display and access in minimum space, connected by stairs on which two people could not pass.' It was a perfect place for children. It was 'their' shop. Eleven-year-old Master Philip Nye expressed his feelings about it in a poem composed for a competition run by the Puffin Club in 1969:

'I've never seen Sir Basil B.,
But he's the bookseller for me.
His shop in the Broad is tall and thin,
With plenty of Puffin books therein.
I imagine him like his bookshop,
Lean and tall with a bowler on top,
With ginger whiskers and horn-rimmed specs,
Sending bills and signing cheques.
On the top floor of his shop, I see,
Are books for older boys like me,
While right at the bottom there are lots
Of picture books for tiny tots.
I wonder if Sir B.'s like that,
With wise old thoughts beneath his hat,
And toddling around on tiny feet,
With a middle-aged middle; he must look sweet.

But in time the department again grew too big for its quarters, and in 1974 the new Children's Bookshop at 6 Broad Street was opened, in a happily chaotic style. Orinoco Womble led a silver band and hundreds of boys and girls to its doors, creating in the process a traffic jam in central Oxford that lasted for two hours.

The design and launching of the new shop were in the hands of Basil's younger son Julian ('Toby'), eleven years Richard's junior, educated, like him, at Winchester (but not as a scholar), and afterwards at Trinity College Oxford. He joined the company in 1952, and one of his special responsibilities became the planning and oversight of major new building operations. The first and, for Blackwell's customers, most conspicuous of these was what is known as the Norrington Room. By the beginning of the sixties the need for more space in Broad Street had become urgent, but there seemed no possible way of providing it sideways or upwards. It was, in the end, provided underground. Blackwell's friendly neighbour, and Toby's old college, Trinity, was also seeking to expand and in 1962 appointed

'ORINOCO' AT THE CHILDREN'S BOOKSHOP WITH JULIAN

two young architects, Robert Maguire and Keith Murray, to draw up plans for the development of the south-eastern corner of the college property, adjoining Blackwell's. In these plans there was provision for an underground area that might solve Blackwell's problems. This simple idea was followed up with enthusiasm by both parties, and led, after much elaboration, to the construction of an enormous subterranean terraced chamber of some 10,000 square feet, with two and a half miles of shelving containing 160,000 volumes. Blackwell's christened the Norrington Room after the then

President of Trinity, and it was formally opened by Sir William Haley, editor of *The Times*, in 1966.

The next project for Julian Blackwell to deal with was also the outcome of co-operation with Trinity. Between No. 51 Broad Street and the little White Horse Inn stood Marriott House, from whose windows Trinity undergraduates had thrown sugar knobs at Britannia so many years ago. It had been severely damaged by death-watch beetle and was to be pulled down. The college decided to put up a new building, the upper floors for undergraduate rooms, as before, but the ground floor to be made available as an extension of Blackwell's main shop. This extension became the Art Bookshop, and was opened in 1966 by the Keeper (now Director) of the National Gallery, (Sir) Michael Levey.

The setting up of a separate Music Department has been described in Chapter XVI. It was housed at first in a diminutive shop in Holy-well, but it prospered so greatly under Dymond's management that

THE OPENING OF THE MUSIC SHOP
Frederick Dymond   The Gaffer   Sir Adrian Boult

The hole in the ground

The room takes shape

THE NORRINGTON ROOM

The finished room

Julian Blackwell   Sir William   Richard Blackwell

OPENED BY SIR WILLIAM HALEY

CONSTRUCTION OF BEAVER HOUSE

BEAVER HOUSE AFTER COMPLETION

a move into more spacious premises became imperative. This time another college, Wadham, came to the rescue. The College was considering plans for the redevelopment of their property along the north side of Holywell, and a site was, in due course, allotted to Blackwell's, next door to their existing music shop. The new Music Shop has a large basement area, reminiscent of the Norrington Room, and holds, as well as thousands of books, over 25,000 items of music, from full orchestral scores to chamber ensembles, and more than 10,000 records and cassettes. This building, too, was formally opened, in 1970, by a distinguished visitor from the outer world, Sir Adrian Boult, an old friend and Oxford contemporary of the Gaffer.

These four new buildings were all initiated, and designed, to promote direct sales from counter to customer. But these now made up only a small part of the firm's turnover. Far the greater part came from mail order sales, combining periodicals, exports, and a large proportion of book sales in the UK. To cope with the growth of these activities, and of the Accounts Division, more and more premises all over Oxford had been acquired, piecemeal, until by the mid sixties there were more than a dozen such outposts. This was inconvenient enough already, and soon still more space would be needed. A plan was suggested by Julian Blackwell and C. P. Wareham, head of the Accounts Division (he was made a Director of the company in 1971), and in 1967 produced its report. It recommended the construction of a new building specially designed to accommodate all the 'backroom' services, including the Periodicals Division. A site was acquired near the station and in 1973 Beaver House was opened, an office block of striking design, the first building to catch the visitor's eye on his way from the railway to the university. The beaver, 'an animal fond of hard work and aquatic pursuits' as the Gaffer said, is not only the family crest and official emblem of Blackwell's but a supporter of the arms of the city of Oxford.

XIX

Publishing since the War: Blackwell and Mott (B & M) and Basil Blackwell Publisher

BEFORE the 1939–1945 war B & M's prosperity was due to their success with children's books and schoolbooks, but after the war these began to fail them. There was at first a drop in the sales of children's books, 'even Enid Blyton's', as Henry Schollick told an almost incredulous Annual General Meeting in 1950, and there was no knowing when that market might recover. In point of fact it recovered very soon, but Henry had by then decided to give up publishing 'juveniles'. Schoolbooks were another matter. They might have their ups and downs but demand could not fail in the long run—and the birth rate was rising. But since the death of E. W. Parker in 1933 there was no one left in B & M with the special experience needed for success in this competitive field. 'Uncle' Henry himself, in any case, had not the time to spare. He was on the board of each component company in the Blackwell group and took an active part in policy-making. He was in charge of the Foreign Department in the shop. He sat on the Council of the Booksellers Association, and was chairman of Book Tokens Ltd. If B & M were to re-enter the educational field new blood was needed.

Accordingly, in 1951 John Cutforth, a former schoolmaster and one of HM Inspectors of Schools, was appointed Educational Editor, and his experience and enthusiasm led to the recovery of lost ground. His chief interest lay in primary education. He inaugurated, for example, the well-known *Learning Library* which, by 1979, contained more than one hundred titles, and he led the way in the production of the teaching cards, wall charts and the like now so widely used in the schools. He had some success too with books for secondary schools, such as M. N. Duffy's *The Twentieth Century*, often re-printed, and he produced a number of valuable books on teaching theory and practice.

John Cutforth was much more than educational editor. His active and sociable personality found expression in many other ways in the Blackwell organization, notably in his enthusiastic inspiration of the Blackwell Singers, who have made a notable contribution to amateur music in Oxford and whose fine singing at the opening of the Music Shop in 1970 moved Sir Adrian Boult to address them as 'dear colleagues'. Since his official retirement in 1976 he keeps up an active contact with the bookselling side of Blackwell's, and edits the *Broad Sheet*.

Henry Schollick (H.L.S., nicknamed 'Heat, Light, and Sound' in Broad Street with mingled awe and affection), was bent on establishing B & M as academic publishers. A small but successful beginning had been made, during the war, with the series of modern language texts mentioned in Chapter XIV. B & M had to make its way in a field strongly held by publishers of high renown, of whom not the least formidable, the OUP, had its headquarters less than a mile away. But Henry was not deterred. Besides, he had two points in his favour. The orders that came into the bookshop from universities at home and abroad provided him with copious and invaluable evidence of market trends; and the big publishers had to give priority to reprinting their standard works to cope with the backlog of orders held over from the war, while B & M, new in the field, were free to promise authors rapid production.

Henry Schollick had read PPE at Oxford and the list he began to build up was naturally strong in Philosophy, Politics, and Economics; in modern languages too, and in theology, his lifelong concern as a staunch and 'liberal' Catholic. In philosophy he won much kudos for his firm by becoming the publisher of Ludwig Wittgenstein, widely recognized as one of the most influential sages of the century. When Wittgenstein died in 1951 he had published only one book, but he left a mass of unpublished material, the editing and translation of which was to occupy scholars for many years and founded what Henry called 'the Wittgenstein industry'.

The academic books that B & M produced secured the reputation of the firm but brought slow returns. More rapidly profitable were some successful books for the general reader, of which the best known in its day was (Sir) Fred Hoyle's *Nature of the Universe* (1950), a series of lectures given on the BBC Third Programme, in which the author put forward an entirely new theory of the origin of the universe. It created a sensation and sold over 100,000 copies before appearing as a Penguin. Fred Hoyle was Richard's discovery.

B & M's turnover did not exceed £100,000 until 1955, but then the growth that Schollick had planned so tenaciously began in earnest. Sixteen years later, when he retired as managing director, the turnover was over £400,000. He was succeeded in 1971 by J. K. D. (Jim) Feather, whom he had taken on as his assistant in 1966—'the perfect colleague' Henry called him. The firm continued to expand and when, in 1976, Jim Feather left to join an American firm in the USA and was in his turn succeeded by David Martin, sales were rising very rapidly. By 1979 they were over £2,000,000.

The foundation of the firm of Blackwell and Mott in 1922 was described in Chapter VII. For many years, however, the imprint used on title-pages had been simply 'Basil Blackwell', with the company's full designation on the verso. This was confusing, and, besides, Sir Adrian Mott had retired some time before he died in 1964. In 1978 the name of the firm was formally changed to Basil Blackwell Publisher.

The binding business had been managed as part of the publishing business ever since its amalgamation with Blackwell and Mott in 1922, and for many years had been producing a substantial part of the combined profits. After the war the binding business expanded rapidly and in 1962 it began a separate existence as the Kemp Hall Bindery Limited, with Julian Blackwell as its first chairman and Geoffrey Barfoot, commemorated in Chapter X, as managing director. A new factory was built at Osney Mead, near the site of the future BSP building, and in 1965 K.H.B. moved in. There Barfoot continued to manage it until his retirement in 1968.

XX

Blackwell Scientific Publications

THE way in which Blackwell Scientific Publications came into being was described in Chapter XIV. The infant firm was making steady but not spectacular progress after the war when, in 1952, a young Dane, Per Saugman, joined it as sales manager. Two years later he succeeded John Grant as managing director. Sales were then running at under £50,000 a year, but an era of extraordinarily rapid and continuous growth was about to begin.

Conditions were, it is true, favourable in a general way. Much material for publication was being produced by the new centres of medical teaching and research in the new universities at home and abroad. By 1960 the number of medical books published in Britain each year was twice as high as before the war and still rising. BSP enjoyed the special advantage of growing up under the wing of the best-known academic booksellers in the world. But the field of medical publishing was strongly held by specialist firms of long standing and great experience. It was no easy matter to gain a foothold in it, and Per Saugman's success was quite remarkable. He combined professionalism and flair with a sense of vocation. His family had distinguished itself in the field of medicine, and Per had always hoped for a career in medical publishing. Now his chance had come and he took it with both hands.

The publication of new knowledge by the best authors was the aim originally set when BSP was founded, but monographs embodying the latest research, however good, have a limited sale. By the time Per joined the firm the directors had decided that their field need no longer be limited to 'pure science and research', though they still had misgivings about actual textbooks because of competi-

PER SAUGMAN

tion with the established publishers. Per had no such misgivings, and today it is on undergraduate and postgraduate textbooks that BSP relies for the bulk of its book sales. The firm published its thousandth book in 1974.

Periodicals have now become as important a source of revenue as books. The first appeared in 1955, the *British Journal of Haematology*, and it was followed during the next twenty-five years by more than fifty others. Their subject matter has not been restricted to medicine, and in time books also have begun to appear in non-medical fields. BSP began life as a solely medical publishing firm, but the term 'scientific' in its title was deliberately adopted in order to leave wider options open. A series of *Botanical Monographs* was initiated in 1962, and in 1968 a biology editor, Robert Campbell, was appointed. Diversification, confined so far to the life sciences, had begun in earnest.

For all his enterprise as a publisher, Saugman has also been a careful and economical manager, and has kept a tight rein on over-heads. In 1979 there were actually fewer people employed in the office than seven years earlier, though sales were seven times as great. Production per capita has been so high that the Department of Industry's Business Statistics Office has had occasion to query Per's figures. These remarkable results could only have been achieved with the support of a well-organized, able, and devoted staff. Keith Bowker, nominally sales and publicity manager, joined the company only one year after his chief, in 1953. His duties are much wider than the formal definition of them suggests. As business expanded the need to strengthen the management team grew. A production manager, John Robson, was appointed in 1961 and a chief account-ant, Peter Pleasance, in 1967. John has maintained the high quality of the imprint aimed at by the firm from its earliest days, and his designs have sometimes been selected by the National Book League as amongst the best fifty of the year. Peter Pleasance saw the turn-over multiply more than fifteen times by 1979 and had to supervise the installation of advanced computerization.

Editorial branches have been set up in Edinburgh and London to make contact with new authors and maintain close links with regular

BSP authors. Nigel Palmer, son of the company secretary of B. H. Blackwell Ltd, was put in charge of the Edinburgh office in 1967, and Per's son Peter in London in 1971.

BSP is linked to a number of companies overseas acquired or set up by Per to promote exports, which in 1979 accounted for nearly three-quarters of the total sales, and to attract authors. In Europe the Danish firm of Ejnar Munksgaard, the largest academic publishing firm, principally of medical books, in Scandinavia, was acquired in 1963. Per took pride, and special care, in reorganizing and modernizing the firm in which he received his first training in the book trade. For his services to publishing in Denmark he has been made a Knight of Dannebrog. A more recent acquisition was the Dutch bookselling and publishing firm of C. Kooyker of Leiden, which led to the founding of Kooyker Scientific Publications in Rotterdam. Two subsidiaries have been set up in Australia to keep in contact with authors and promote export sales. In the USA a partnership with the C. V. Mosby company came into effect on 1 January 1979, which was designed to improve BSP's share of the American market.

Per Saugman is chairman of the most self-contained and independent of the Blackwell companies, and the BSP building seems to proclaim this status by its situation on the outskirts of Oxford and by the individuality of its design. The rapid growth of the company in the sixties led to a decision to solve the problems of space, once for all, by providing an ample new building, and a site was chosen at Osney, with a fine view across the Thames of the Oxford skyline. Per knew what he wanted and worked in close collaboration with his architects, the Oxford Architects Copartnership. The result is a distinguished building that combines comfortable working conditions with economic efficiency. It was opened in May 1972, the headquarters of an international publishing company with an unrivalled reputation for the skilfulness of its management and the quality of its products. By 1979 the annual turnover was approaching £7 million.

XXI

Bookselling since the War:
Thirty Years of Soaring Growth

THE last third of Blackwell's first century was a period marked by such rapid inflation that £10 million in 1979 was worth little more, in real terms, than £1 million in 1945. But the turnover of Blackwell's bookselling business multiplied during those years, not by ten, but by over one hundred and sixty. This startling result was due to the adoption and energetic application of new techniques of salesmanship to take advantage of what has been called the explosion in education, especially tertiary education, and especially overseas. There are no very reliable statistics for the growth of the world student population since the war, but in Britain, for example, more than twenty new universities came into being and by 1979 the student population had increased fivefold. In some countries the increase was even greater. Richard Blackwell had his eye on this market when, in 1949, he put forward his proposals for reorganization, but to get the fullest possible benefit from reorganization one thing more was needed, personal contacts with customers abroad.

This need was not, to be sure, self-evident. The name and reputation of the firm were well established abroad, so well that a correspondent in New York could write to Henry Schollick in 1962 that 'an account at Blackwell's is very much a status symbol in university, college and seminary circles here'. This enviable reputation had not been won by visiting customers on their home grounds —though some of them had, indeed, been to Oxford. All this was about to change. In 1961 the Gaffer made a pioneering journey to South Africa in pursuit of trade, but the real turning-point came two

MILES B.B. NIGEL RICHARD JULIAN

years later when Richard set out for the American Library Association Conference in Chicago, accompanied by his personal assistant Joyce Ferguson and seen off by his colleagues on what then seemed a novel enterprise. The enterprise proved highly rewarding, and soon overseas travel became a commonplace, and essential, means of promoting and cementing business relations.

George Bunting became Director in charge of the export department in 1964, and in the same year found his department involved in the first of a series of large contracts for the supply of books to newly equipped libraries in North Africa and the Middle East. His frequent visits to arrange for the handling of these contracts earned him the nickname of Bunting Pasha. By 1970 export sales (including periodicals) had risen from £60,000 in 1946 to over £4,700,000 and were accounting for two-thirds of the firm's turnover.

Meanwhile Miles Blackwell, Richard's elder son, had joined the family firm in 1966 and began to follow in the footsteps of the Pasha and his father. He took a leading part, for example, in building a special, and very fruitful, relationship with libraries in the Arabian Peninsula. One consignment of books filled a Boeing 707 freighter. When Bunting retired in 1974, Miles became a Director of the company, in charge of what was designated the Mail Order Division. In the last five years of the Blackwell century the sales of the Division rose faster than ever, Mail Order had become much the largest part of the bookselling business, and the policy recommended by Miles's father thirty years earlier had been amply vindicated.

Retail sales had, since Hine's retirement in 1964, been managed by the redoubtable C. S. (Sam) Knights, who became a Director of the company in 1967. He remained, till the day of his death in 1972, a traditional all-round bookseller, one of the last of the breed, no 'specialist'. He was succeeded by his brother Harry, also a Director since 1967, and after his retirement in 1974 Richard's younger son Nigel became Director or the Retail Division. He brought a fresh mind to bear on the management of the shops, and under his leadership innovations were accepted that proved greatly to the benefit of the retail business but would perhaps have been viewed with misgivings by his more conservative predecessors.

The way in which George's Bookshop in Bristol became part of the Blackwell group in 1929, and its remarkable growth during the war, have already been described. After the war other bookshops in the west country were taken under its wing to form a regional group that became one of the foremost in the provinces. In the sixties a new initiative was taken by Richard Blackwell in the interests of regional bookselling. Bookshops in some university towns were finding it difficult to meet the needs of the new academic populations. They had been used to catering for a smaller and less specialized local demand, and they needed more capital and more expertise. Richard accordingly approached the Oxford University Press, and a consortium was set up in 1964 to enter into partnership with existing bookshops which needed support, and University Bookshops (Oxford) Ltd. (UBO) began. It soon proved its worth, and in 1970 Eric Bailey, Treasurer, and later President, of the Booksellers' Association, was brought in as group managing director. The first chairman of the Board, which consisted of an equal number of representatives of the OUP and Blackwell's, was Dr John Thomson, chairman of the finance committee of the OUP, and on his death in 1975 he was succeeded by Sir John Brown, then the OUP London Publisher. The aim of enhancing the standard of regional academic bookselling had been achieved.

XXII

The Private Company shows
its Strength

A STRIKING proof of the confidence felt by the outside world
in the strength of the Blackwell Group came in the mid
seventies. An American firm, the Richard Abel Company of
Oregon, had, since its foundation in the fifties, became an out-
standingly successful worldwide supplier of books and periodicals
to libraries and other institutions, but by 1974 it had run into difficulties. Abel had gone too far in undercutting competitors to secure
trade, and had overreached himself. For a last chance of survival he
turned to Blackwell's. A team from Oxford was despatched to
Oregon to look into the affairs or the Company with the help of an
expert group of North American librarians and booksellers, but they
could see no hope of its survival. At Abel's own suggestion, however, Miles Blackwell and a colleague, John Pigott, were left behind
to work out with the creditors a financial plan to buy those assets of
the Abel Company necessary for the creation of a new business, and
on 27 January 1975 Blackwell North America Inc. came into being.

The Blackwell Group was already one of the greatest bookselling
businesses in the world, and one of the most complex. The accession
of BNA, the largest subsidiary in the Group, added greatly to the
responsibilities of central control, of decision-making at the top, in
effect to the burden of the Chief Executive, Richard Blackwell, who
had been designated Managing Director in 1966 and had succeeded
his father as Chairman in 1969. David Ellis, an expert in finance
management, was brought in as Managing Director in 1975 to
lighten the Chairman's load, but spent less than three years with the
Company before leaving to take up another post in the book trade,

and this central problem of the delegation of responsibilities was still unsolved when Richard Blackwell's serious illness came upon him in 1978.

In small businesses the post of Company Secretary may be little more than the name implies. The Secretary is the man who writes and keeps the records of board meetings. But in complex businesses the post may become of central importance. The Secretary's records cover the activities of a number of distinct, though related, boards, and he is thus the man best placed to keep the internal lines of communication open. He can give warning of gaps or overlaps in the total organization, and offer advice about the effect the plans of one section of the business may have on the others. These functions have been performed, during the years leading up to the Blackwell Centenary, by C. A. ('Uncle') Palmer, whose firm sagacity has sometimes caused him to be called 'the conscience of the Company'. He came into the firm in 1953 as Chief Accountant, and on his promotion to be Company Secretary was succeeded as head of the Accounts Division by C. P. ('George') Wareham. Wareham came to Blackwell's from the Cambridge University Press as Palmer's assistant, and was jointly responsible, with Julian Blackwell, as we have seen, for producing the report which led to the centralization of services in Beaver House.

At the end of its first century Blackwell's was still a private company. A consistent policy of retaining profits in the business and shunning extravagance had enabled the firm to achieve its remarkable growth without the infusion of capital from outside. But vigilance was needed after the war to mitigate the worst effects of legislation that sometimes seemed designed to discourage, or even prevent, the accumulation of capital. The firm's professional adviser in these matters, fiscal and legal, has been John Critchley, whose father Harry (who died in 1959) was one of the founding directors of B. H. Blackwell Ltd., and for some thirty years the friend, confidant, and counseller of the Gaffer, and of his father before him. The family, and the firm, owe much to the wisdom and ability of these two generations of Critchleys.

Richard Blackwell was passionately concerned to defend the

private business, whose capacity for effort and enterprise he saw as a bulwark against the decline of Britain, and with John Critchley he helped to found the Small Businesses Association, which later developed into the Association of Independent Businesses. A measure introduced by Chancellor Roy Jenkins during the second Labour government of the 1960s struck him, and a good many others, as a particularly irritating, not to say useless, piece of bureaucratic interference. It insisted upon disclosure of the minutest financial details of a company's working pattern, 'omitting no detail however trivial', as Sherlock Holmes used to say. Julian suggested that much private information about the firm could be withheld from revelation to the authorities by forming a Management Company. Only the chairman need provide information about his private affairs in relation to the company, but the title of the new company must not reveal the name of the company managed. Any other title might be adopted. Gaffer and Richard settled for the title U. P. Jenkins Ltd. The Registrar, on receiving the application, asked, 'Is there a Jenkins in the enterprise?' 'Oh yes', answered Blackwell's, giving the name of the solicitor who was advising them as to the Articles of Association and acting as a director. The objects of U. P. Jenkins Ltd. were stated to be, among other things, 'to erect, construct, lay down, enlarge, alter and maintain any roads, railways, tramways, sidings, bridges, reservoirs, shops, stores, factories, buildings, works, plant and machinery necessary or convenient for the Company's business'.

This breezy disrespect for state control was matched by an equally spirited devotion to the traditional values he had learned to admire and revere in boyhood and youth, not least the value of the classics. The following account of Richard's admiration put into practice, the *Musarum Restitutio* in 1974, has been contributed by Christopher Francis.

'It has long been a pious tradition at Blackwell's that the Gaffer was born in his office. Though this makes a better story, he was in fact born in the room above and for some thirty-four years this room was occupied by Richard Blackwell. From his desk in the corner he looked out every day upon the roof of the Clarendon

Building, then the very heart of the University, designed by Hawksmoor and built in 1711 to 1713, partly out of the profits of Clarendon's *History of the Rebellion*, to serve as a New Printing House. In 1717, according to Hearne, they received "a Parcell of Heavy leaden statues call'd the nine Muses". These had been designed by Sir James Thornhill but "had lain at ye wharf for two years having been first of all refused". The original price of £600 may have been in dispute, for the University, by some nice bargaining, eventually acquired them for £300 and they were installed on the roof of the building, a fitting symbol of the spirit of the University. Whatever may have happened to them in the next two centuries, how they endured the weather, or if any collapsed under her weight —*mole ruit sua*—or if Melpomene in particular suffered her own tragedy through some plumbic *hamartia* we cannot say, but we do know that one collapsed and fell in 1897 and another about fifteen years later, leaving an unfortunate gap with Euterpe and Melpomene no longer there and the unity of the arts thus broken.

'In 1973 it seemed to Richard Blackwell that it would be, in view of our debt to the University and our work in promoting the arts, a fitting gesture if we offered to replace the missing ladies. The offer was gratefully accepted, sketches of the original were discovered by Robert Potter in Worcester College Library, and two new ladies were made by Richard Kindersley Image Workshops, in reinforced glass fibre, resin-finished with lead.

'On June 6th, 1974, they were solemnly unveiled with a delightful ceremony of speech and music in the Sheldonian in the presence of the Vice-Chancellor and presided over by that *vir Irreverendus* brought back from earlier centuries, Terrae Filius, revived with great wit by Graham Midgley. The University Orchestra played appropriately Handel's Overture to *Athalia* and Haydn's Oxford Symphony No. 92 in G. Both composers were present in full costume in the person of John Cutforth as an impressive Handel and Willy Brown of Parker's as a convincing Haydn, fresh from his honorary degree of Doctor of Music in 1791. Edward East was wholly authentic as the antiquary Hearne and other parts were suitably played.

THE MUSES RESTORED

From left to right: Graham Midgley, John Cutforth, R.B., Edward East, James Sabben-Clare,
the trumpeter, Willy Brown, John Owen

'Terrae Filius described the occasion and paid tribute to Richard Blackwell in a speech of sparkling good-humour and two Winchester colleagues, the Sabben-Clares, *pater et filius*, celebrated the event, the one in English and the other in Latin verse. But no such occasion would have been complete without a piece of elegant Latin from the Public Orator, John Griffith, a great friend of the Firm.

'This was a very civilized occasion in the best traditions of Blackwell's and the University and greatly enjoyed. For Richard Blackwell it was a symbol of his own deep concern for our classical heritage and his interest in the arts and it aptly summed up the close relationship between the shop and the University and underlined the fact that, however much the Firm might have grown and extended itself far and wide, it never lost sight of its origins in and its obligations to its own University of Oxford.'

XXIII

1979: The Centenary Year[1]

I F, from the Elysian fields, we could summon to the door of
50 Broad Street the shade of Benjamin Henry Blackwell, what
thoughts would pass through his mind one hundred years on
from the modest launching of the business he founded? Might he
climb the stairs and halt reflectively at the top of the old building,
in that room where three times a day he had said his prayers? Would
he not marvel, recalling the cramped premises in which Blackwell's
had its beginnings, at the thousands upon thousands of books around
him on the shop floors; at the vastness of the Norrington Room; at
the wonders of technology, which in the late twentieth century
translate his painstaking study of the Quaritch Catalogue into computer terminals on which any member of the staff with a few hours'
training can call up instant information on the half-million titles in
the computerized file at Beaver House? We can imagine his satisfaction and pride in seeing that his aims of excellence and good
service should have led to Beaver House, to Basil Blackwell Publisher, to Blackwell Scientific Publications, to today's multiplicity
of interests at home and abroad, and to the many members of
Blackwell's who have worked and still serve in the enterprise which
sprang from his lonely efforts.

Let us follow him. He is drawn down Broad Street, through
Radcliffe Square, across the High (in which nowadays no weeds
live, as in the Long Vacation a century ago, nor any present-day
pedestrian who dare tarry in his crossing), and into the Chapel of
Merton. For this is 3 January, and his spirit must be with the congregation come together to celebrate and give thanks for the

---

[1] This account of the Centenary is by three members of Blackwell's family.

Centenary. That celebration and thanksgiving, in the presence of the Chancellor of the University, Harold Macmillan, and the Vice-Chancellor, Sir Rex Richards, was an affirmation of the tradition of 'godliness and good learning', which has always been a part of the ethos of both family and firm. It was also fitting that it should be held in a College chapel, underlining Blackwell's close connection with the seat of learning which surrounds it, and that the particular location should be Merton, the Gaffer's own college, of which Sir Rex is Warden.

Those who were near the entrance will not quickly forget that moment when the Gaffer came to greet the Chancellor, and they stood together under the arch as two representatives—one of the University, both of the world of books—venerable alike in age and achievement. The hymns and prayers had been well chosen for the occasion, marking in turn gratitude for past accomplishments and reaffirmation of endeavour in time to come:

We have met to give thanks to God for his goodness to us throughout the one hundred years of Blackwell's life, and to pray for His continued blessing on our labours.

... Grant that we may work with wisdom and strength and that out of a knowledge of the past, we may fulfil our obligations to the future ... and be of service to Thy people in times to come.

We pray for all those who publish books and by their labour enable research, teaching and learning to continue ... for the good purpose of education and ... stewardship of the benefits of Thy creation.

... Direct ... those who write and publish what many will read: that they may do their part in making the heart of this people wise, its mind sound, and its will righteous.

The Blackwell Singers, surely the oldest surviving and most successful of our Societies, sang—all too briefly—a short anthem from the works of Adrian Batten, 'O sing joyfully unto God our strength'.

The most moving moment for many occurred when the Gaffer walked to the lectern, and the voice so often heard in other celebrations of the past rose to this greater occasion with a reading of the Lesson, the familiar passage from Ecclesiasticus: 'Let us now praise famous men and our fathers that begat us.' In these words were commemorated all those who made the gathering possible: the family, from the Founder's father, Benjamin Harris Blackwell, who died so young but left his ideal for his son to pursue, to the newest generation of Miles and Nigel, upon whom rests the challenge of the future; and all the staff, who through the century made their vital contribution to the building of the prestige and achievement to which the day was dedicated.

After the Service, Merton Hall was filled with members of Blackwell's, luminaries of the University and guests from publishing, bookselling, and other professions, to observe the commemoration of the Centenary in a different and tangible form. Blackwell's has long acknowledged its debt to the world of learning, and over the years has sought, in the establishment of the Nancy Stirling Lambert and James Cook scholarships, to do something in return for librarians and the profession of librarianship. In Merton Hall, after Harold Macmillan's witty and nostalgic speech in which he talked of his belief in private companies 'doing our best for country, Church and people, if we work honestly and well', Richard Blackwell and Per Saugman announced the repayment of the hundred-year debt to the University of Oxford. It took the shape of a benefaction of £350,000 to St. Cross College, one of the new graduate Societies established by the University in 1965 and housed hitherto in temporary quarters in Holywell, but which would now be enabled to move into the middle of Oxford and share the buildings of Pusey House.

The year 1979 saw also another anniversary, for in the year of the firm's centenary the Gaffer celebrated his ninetieth birthday. His energy and vital interest in the affairs of Blackwell's, and the world outside, remained unimpaired by the years. He was still coming to the office every day, though he had given up—but only very recently—his habit of taking stairs two at a time. The secret of his longevity is not easy to determine. He has been wont to say that it can be ascribed to 'being in a constant state of mild irritation', or to portray himself

BASIL BLACKWELL, 1979

as the acrobat on top of a human pyramid—'everybody is doing his best to support me; I am supporting no one, but smiling and accepting the applause'. And he has suggested that his greatest achievement over a long life is 'never being found out!'

The Gaffer has received many honours. He is the first and only bookseller to be knighted. He has an Honorary D.Litt. from the University of Manchester, he is an Honorary Freeman of the Stationers' Company, he was awarded the Freedom of the City of Oxford, and, most cherished of all, he holds an Honorary Fellowship of Merton. On 27 June 1979, the University paid its homage at Encaenia in the Sheldonian Theatre to this 'Jupiter of Booksellers', as the address had it, when the Gaffer received an Honorary Doctorate of Civil Law, and walked in the procession in the company of Graham Greene, whose first publisher he had been.

The love and affection which has surrounded the Gaffer so long found its expression for staff, customers, and bookselling and publishing colleagues in two parties in the grounds of Trinity College in July, and most notably at a concert held at Blenheim Palace, when noble music and an equally noble setting combined to produce a memorable celebration of both his birthday and the Centenary itself.

Epilogue

No cloud should have come to darken the Centenary year, but, alas, throughout that year Richard's family and his closest friends watched a shadow come closer and grow darker. Symptoms of a fatal malady had appeared in 1978, and during 1979 the hateful truth declared itself. Richard Blackwell worked on, undaunted, to the end. On 26 February 1980 he died. He had celebrated the Centenary. He had just passed his sixty-second birthday.

His life's work in enhancing the prosperity of the family firm already made famous by his father and his grandfather has been described. We have learned something of what he did. Now that he has gone it is right to try to say something of what he was—without impertinence, for, as Henry Schollick said in his moving address at the memorial service in the University church of St. Mary on 15 March 1980, Richard was 'a very private person'. It was not his way to talk about himself and he looked for, and respected, such reticence in others. He was a man of exceptional modesty, but very sure of his aims and very tenacious in pursuing them. This combination of qualities may have been in part responsible for the impression he gave some people of having difficulty in communicating easily; self-confidence warring with self-deprecation. It made him a difficult person to know.

We catch a valuable and endearing glimpse of young Richard Blackwell in the war from one of his old shipmates. 'In moments of danger he was totally unruffled.' Unruffled, but on the look-out for improving the occasion with a little judicious levity. 'On the bridge I would receive a heavily sealed "Hush! Most Secret" envelope with some scurrilous but extremely apt and witty composition to amuse himself and me.'

The last months of Richard Blackwell's life revealed his exemplary

fortitude. When Henry Schollick saw him for the last time he said to him, 'You have fought a good fight.' 'I *am* fighting a good fight', Richard replied. He showed no self-pity. He struck no attitude. He never stopped trying.

Index